A NOISE OF MUSIC

ALAN R. WARWICK

A NOISE OF MUSIC

QUEEN ANNE PRESS
in association with
THE CORPORATION OF LONDON

*Made and printed in Great Britain for the Queen Anne
Press Limited of 49 Poland Street, London W.1 by
Tonbridge Printers Limited, Tonbridge, Kent.*

FOREWORD

by

Sir Gilbert Inglefield, T.D., M.A.

I like the title of this splendid book – 'A Noise of Music' – for the music heard in the City of London has varied enormously from the primitive sounds of Saxon gleemen to concerts in Guildhall by the London Symphony Orchestra. If only the tape recorder had been in use in the middle ages! However learned the musicologist may be – and surely Mr Warwick is among the most scholarly and erudite – neither he nor we can ever know what the shawms and recorders, the drums and the sackbuts of the City waits really sounded like, or what technical skill the players exercised.

If it were possible to be translated back in time to some episode in history, to be present for a few minutes, what would one choose? To see Tamburlane ride in triumph through Persepolis? To watch King John sign Magna Carta? To observe Louis XIV at Versailles or Charles I being executed? To be with Nelson at Trafalgar or Wellington at Quatre Bras?

No! I would ask for just five minutes, or if possible a quarter of an hour, in Neal's Music Hall in Dublin's Fishamble Street at the first performance of 'Messiah'. I should then know for certain what Handel's tempi were in the solos, what the balance of the orchestra was like, and if Mrs Cibber's voice was as good as her interpretation; if the standard of musicianship was as high as it was supposed to be, what appoggiature were employed, and how the choruses sounded. If I couldn't get to Ireland, then a few minutes at the first performance in London of the last movement of Beethoven's Ninth Symphony with the composer, by then, stone deaf, sitting in the front row. Was the woodwind in tune? Was it really taken as Presto? Did the brass always come in at the right bar? Alas, we shall never know.

However, we can learn a great deal from literary and critical research. We can almost recapture from these pages the scenes and the sounds that went on in the City's streets. Gone today are the cries of vendors, but as a boy in the West End of London, I can remember hearing the tinkle of the muffin man's bell, and being encouraged to buy lavender from an itinerant soprano.

This story is concerned, too, with individual people, some of whom were to have an important influence. Robert Hubert, alias Forges, the inn-keeper of the 'Mitre' (near St Paul's) and Edmund Chilmead of the 'Black Horse' in Aldersgate, were pioneers in the City. So too was the anoymous publican of another 'Mitre', in Wapping, of which there is a lively if slender description given by Ned Ward. There was a club in Old Jewry to which Playford dedicated an edition of his compositions, – yet more important was John Banister's venture in Whitefriars, for here was the first important concert hall mentioned by Roger North.

But of all the early impresarios the most endearing character was surely the 'small coal' man of Clerkenwell, Thomas Britton, who lived on the edge of the City. His end was rather sad. A friend, who was a ventriloquist, played him a practical joke by telling him in a strange voice that he was soon to die. This so frightened the poor little man that he fell into a nervous decline and died. Surely he is worthy of a monument somewhere in Clerkenwell near the site of his humble loft?

The 17th century was a golden age when English music and English musicians were big exports, but I believe that in 1968 English music is beginning to reach new heights.

This is reflected in the City. After a lapse of many years, the City is becoming a very important patron of the Arts, and of music in particular. There is now a biennial City Festival, and when the Arts Centre in the Barbican project has been realised – let us hope within the next few years, – there will be a new Theatre where Shakespeare may find once again a place within the square mile. A new concert hall will, in all probability, be the home of the London Symphony Orchestra – the first permanent home any great London orchestra has ever had. And between the theatre and the concert hall the Guild-hall School of Music is to find new premises.

The City again begins to resound with music. Who knows? Perhaps the London Symphony Orchestra may once again become the rein-carnation of the Old City Waits. Why should they not be the City Waits themselves? If this happens old Ned Ward's description of those haphazard musicians of the 17th century will certainly not be applicable. Sir Arthur Bliss recently wrote an invigorating 'Fanfare for the Lord Mayor', first played by the London Symphony Orchestra this year. Is this a prophetic gesture?

CONTENTS

ILLUSTRATIONS

Taken from the History of the Coronation of James II, printed by Thomas Newcombe, one of His Majesty's Printers, 1687. The whole work is illustrated by several 'sculptures' (engravings), of which this illustration is part. The artist was Nicholas Yeates, and the illustration shows trumpets and kettle-drums as an item of the Coronation Procession.

In the History is the description '. . . the Drums Beat a March and the Trumpets sounded several Levets, and the Choirs sang all the way.'

ACKNOWLEDGMENTS

In this excursion into the musical past of the City of London, I have been most fortunate in the help I have received from so many quarters. First and foremost, I must express my most sincere thanks to the Lord Mayor, Alderman Sir Gilbert Inglefield, T.D., M.A., for his very practical help and encouragement in this exploration, which is so close to his own musical interests. Sir Gilbert has made available to me his own unique collection of musical treasures on which to draw. Thus, the jacket of this book reproduces two pages from the original published score of Handel's *Rinaldo*, from Sir Gilbert's collection. The charming Concert Invitation Cards, and the seldom seen portrait of Thomas Britton, the Musical Small Coal Man, are from the same source.

The assistance I have received from the Worshipful Company of Musicians of London through the kindness and very practical help given me by its Clerk, Brigadier H. A. F. Crewdson, T.D., M.A., has been invaluable. Brigadier Crewdson also gave me free access to his scholarly *History of the Musicians Company*. He has since read the proofs of this book and made useful observations, for which I am most grateful.

I am also indebted to Mr Eric Day, Secretary of the Guildhall School of Music and Drama. Most enthusiastically he contributed with information concerning the history of that great musical establishment. My thanks go also to the School Librarian and members of the staff, who were very helpful.

At Armoury House, Bunhill Fields, home of the Honourable Artillery Company, my enquiry into the Regiment's musical history and its peculiar relation to the City was most courteously received. Lt Colonel P. Massey, M.C., gave me access to much concerning that unique military unit, whose elder brethren provide the Lord Mayor with his guard of pikemen and their drumbeaters.

Concerning the Barbican development with its ambitious plans for the betterment of the City as a cultural and artistic centre, I have to thank Deputy Eric Wilkins, C.B.E., Chairman of the Barbican Committee, for his genial assistance in presenting me with the scheme of things for that once desolate site, or, to use his own words, 'Giving the City a new heart.' In this great undertaking the inspiration of the past and the inspiration for the future are closely welded.

The Guildhall Library became my frequent and ultimate refuge in this search for the City's musical origins, Mr Godfrey Thompson, F.L.A., Guildhall Librarian, the Deputy Librarian, Mr John Bromley, F.L.A., F.S.A., and Members of the Guildhall Library Staff were heart-warming in their painstaking interest in this matter. Their instant grasp of what I wanted to know, and their facility for producing what was required, fills me with respect and warmest thanks. Nodding – as I sometimes did – over the literary and pictorial treasures of London's history that were spread before me on the solid table, I would from time to time find that even more treasures had been silently laid there for my inspection.

While on the subject of City records, it would be remiss of me if I did not make mention of my own City Company, the Worshipful Company of Upholders, who first educated me in that subtle thing, City appreciation. Many of my senior fellow Liverymen, and, not the least among them, the Upholders' erstwhile Clerk, and a Past Master, Mr Ulick J. Burke, directed my tastes to a love of London's historic past and the desire to delve therein. Ulick Burke introduced me to the ramifications of the City Letter Books, from which so much information may be extracted, and sometimes, frustratingly withheld. When Clerk to the Company he showed me several black iron boxes, which held the ancient records of the Company. Those old scrolls and papers, brittle, somewhat charred by fire, somewhat stained by water, suddenly brought to me whispers of a London of earlier ages, with its fire and upheavals, and of events which in their own day were as lively and robust as our own. Incidentally, I am glad to say that those ancient records are no longer in those old iron boxes, but are beautifully restored and safely housed in the Guildhall Library for the veneration of posterity.

I am deeply grateful to all those, both named and unnamed, who have helped me to compile this book, for they have made the quest a gay and enjoyable one. I trust that the result may be thought to be in some degree worthy of all the kindness and help I have been given.

Finally, I thank my publisher, Mr Robert Owen, who so kindly invited me to undertake this work.

A.R.W.

CHAPTER I

TRUMPET BLASTS AND PAGEANTRY

Music in the City of London is like Topsy – it just growed! From the Saxon gleemen who performed on their crude and simple instruments down to the present day, there stretches that unbroken line of descent, which has given London its own peculiar quality – a oneness with itself – that befits every civic occasion, whether of triumph or loss, long-planned or impromptu. City pageantry and tradition are probably without their equal in their maturity and sophistication. Read, for example, the following instructions as issued from the City Remembrancer's Office, Guildhall:

'The Lord Mayor, Aldermen and Sheriffs in their Scarlet Gowns, and the Officers in their Gowns, will leave the Mansion House at 8.30, and proceed to the site of Temple Bar, the Lord Mayor first, and the Aldermen, Sheriffs, and Officers following according to seniority, the whole preceded by the City Trumpeters.

'They will take up their station opposite to the entrance to the Temple, where they will await the arrival of the Pursuivant, Heralds, Officials of Westminster, and Cavalcade, who will have proceeded from St James's Palace.

'A temporary barrier will be placed across the street at the site of Temple Bar to mark the City Boundary.

'The Pursuivant, Heralds and Cavalcade on arriving will halt a short distance to the West of the Barrier. The Pursuivant will advance between two Trumpeters, and the Trumpets will sound thrice.

'The City Marshal will advance to the barrier (on horseback) to meet the Pursuivant, and will ask in a loud voice: "Who comes there?" and the Pursuivant will reply: "The Officer of Arms, who demands entrance into the City to proclaim His Royal Majesty . . . '

'The barrier will then be opened so as to admit the Pursuivant, without escort, and immediately closed again.

'The Pursuivant will be conducted by the City Marshal to the Lord Mayor, who being then acquainted with the object of the Pursuivant's visit, will direct the opening of the barrier, and the Pursuivant will return to his Cavalcade.

'The Officials of Westminster will then file off, and the Cavalcade advance into the City as far as the corner of Chancery Lane.

'The Herald, between two Trumpeters, will approach the Lord Mayor and present to his Lordship the Order in Council requiring him to proclaim His Majesty.

'The Lord Mayor will reply: "I am aware of the contents of this paper, having been apprised yesterday of the Ceremony appointed to take place, and I have attended to perform my duty in accordance with the ancient usages and customs of the City of London.'

'The Lord Mayor will then read aloud the Order in Council requiring the Herald to proclaim His Majesty within the jurisdiction of the City, and return it to the Herald.

'After the trumpets have sounded, the Herald will make the Proclamation.

'Upon the conclusion of the Proclamation, the trumpets will again sound, and the Cavalcade, followed by the Lord Mayor, Aldermen, Sheriffs and Officers, will proceed to the Royal Exchange, where the Proclamation will again be made.

'The Officers of Arms will then be entertained at the Mansion House by the Lord Mayor.'

Within the City these fanfares, together with the colour and the circumstances surrounding the Proclaiming of the Sovereign's Accession are in accordance with the ancient usages and customs. The first trumpet notes are directed across the boundary that separates the City of London from the City of Westminster.

The sound of trumpets come like a glittering shout, but only serve to underline the jealously preserved independence of a City master of itself in all matters, even when pertaining to the Accession of Monarchs.

And when the pageantry is over then comes the homely touch – 'The Officers of Arms will then be entertained at the Mansion House by the Lord Mayor.'

The Ceremony of the Proclamation of the Accession makes a splendid contrast to the starkly sombre note of mourning that is struck when the Secretary of State for Home Affairs informs the Lord Mayor of the demise of the Sovereign, concluding with the bleak words: 'I have to request your Lordship will give directions for tolling the Great Bell of St Paul's Cathedral,' after which the Lord Mayor, having placed himself in communication with the Dean of St Paul's, the Great Bell of the Cathedral is tolled in accordance with precedent.

Whatever the circumstance may be, whether it calls for the sound of trumpets or the tolling of a bell, a Royal Entry or the Lord Mayor's Show, great occasions and triumphs, mournings for things lost, 'the noise of music' has from early times been part and parcel of the sinews of the City of London, both in its ceremonial and in its daily round.

The details vary from age to age, but the music and ceremonial is always there. How charming and tender is the account made at the time of the Great Progress of Queen Elizabeth I through the City immediately before her Coronation. It was a younger London than it is today. It was a London that had just passed through the unhappy reign of Mary. The City turned eagerly to the young and beautiful Elizabeth, daughter of the ill-starred Anne Boleyn.

Records tell us that at Fenchurch there had been raised in her honour a richly decorated scaffold on which stood 'a noyse of instruments', while a child in costly apparel stood to the front to welcome the Queen on behalf of the whole City. At Cornhill, on another platform was another child to welcome her, while a group of musicians played 'heavenly music'.

These are the words of an eye-witness:

'Entrying the Citie [Elizabeth] was of the People received marveylous entirely as appeared by thassemblie, prayers, wishes, welcomings, cryes, tender woordes, and all other signes.

'And on thother syde, her grace, by holding up her handes, and merrie countenance to such as stode farre off, and most tender and gentle language to those that stood nigh to her grace, did declare herselfe no lesse thankfullye to receive her peoples good wyll, than they lovingly offred it unto her . . . so that on eyther syde there was nothing but gladness, nothing but prayer, nothing but comfort.'

And at every station in this Great Progress through the City was the music of choirs and musicians, even to Temple Bar.

It was thirty years after her first youthful entry, that in 1588 Elizabeth came to St Paul's to return thanks for the defeat of the Armada. She was met at Temple Bar by the Lord Mayor, Aldermen and Livery Companies to escort her to the Cathedral. The music of the City Waits played to her from the top of the Bar.

In 1547, in his tenth year, Edward VI was received in the City on his Coronation visit. The gate at Temple Bar was painted to outline battlements, and was richly hung with cloth of arras, and embellished with fourteen standards. Standing on top of the Bar were eight French trumpeters, who, at the boy King's approach sounded a fanfare in the French manner. There was also a pair of regalles (a small organ), to which children sang.

The 'heavenly melodies', the 'singing of angels', the 'noyse of instruments', the 'goodly harmony' – these characterised the Royal Entries into the City in times past. The style was, that as the processions went through the streets they were received and honoured with music and singing by carefully positioned groups of musicians and singers. On the other hand, with town shows and marching watches, and other civic celebrations, minstrels were an important part of the procession. In the place of the stationary platforms, so much a feature of Royal Entries, the platforms with their performers were an integral part of the procession, as are the modern floats of today. In addition to minstrels, and jugglers performing their antics, giant figures were also carried along, representing Gog and Magog and other legendary folk-figures. Giants were immensely popular.

When Henry VIII called upon the City to do honour to Anne Boleyn, who was about to be his bride, the City undertook to furnish three pageants in her honour when she came to the City. One was to be at Leadenhall, a second at the Standard in Cheap, a third at the Little Conduit in Cheap. The pageants were to be on high stages, which were to be 'goodly hanged and garnished with minstrelcy and children singing.'

The Corporation, it should be noted, did not hesitate to ask that they might borrow the King's minstrels for the occasion, to augment their own.

On May 19, 1533 the City Guilds with their banners displayed, occupied fifty great barges, and each barge had its quota of minstrels 'making sweet harmony'. Preceding the Lord Mayor's barge was a galley bearing a huge dragon spouting fire and shooting out fireworks. Every Guild craft followed in its right order of precedence in this lavish water procession to Greenwich to meet and honour the new queen.

The records tell us that when Anne Boleyn went through the City a costly fountain set up at the Great Conduit at Cheap spouted red wine and white wine in great plenty all the afternoon.

The Cross was newly guilded, and there was music and declamations of welcome. At the lesser Conduit a rich pageant was staged 'whereat was goodly harmony of music both instrumental and vocal'.

Ludgate, according to the records, was resplendent in gold, colours and azure, 'with sweet harmony of ballads to her great praise and honour with divers sweet instruments'. The Conduit in Fleet Street was freshly painted and decorated. A choir of 'angels' sang from it, and the fountain ran with claret all the afternoon. Singing men and children stood on Temple Bar, which had been repaired and redecorated for the occasion.

It was in the early thirteenth century that the City of London became possessed of its first Mayor, granted to it by King John. Prior to then the City had been governed by Bailiffs acting for the King.

This meant a fundamental change of the greatest importance, and a recognition of the City's independence. At times subsequently, when the City fell from favour, its mayor was taken from it and the Bailiffs substituted, but never for long. The first Mayor, Henry Fitz-Alwin was, it appears, sworn into office between the years 1192-1211. He was succceeded by Roger Fitz Alan. In 1215 King John granted a Charter, and it was from that date that the appointment of Mayor was recognized by the Crown.

When John granted the City its Mayor he laid it down that whoever was chosen by the citizens for that office should be presented to him for his approval, or, alternatively, to the King's Justices who sat in the Palace of Westminster. It was from this early stipulation making it obligatory for the Mayor to present himself to the King that the world-famous Lord Mayor's Procession was evolved.

In those early days the newly elected Mayor, strongly accompanied by the leading officers of the City and members of the crafts, was accustomed to make his way from the City to Westminster Palace on horseback. Those processions were called Ridings. It was only much later, when pageantry was added, that the term 'Show' or 'Triumph' was adopted.

By the year 1251 the Mayor was no longer called upon to present himself to the King, but to the 'baronys' of the 'exchekyr', who received the oath of allegiance on the King's behalf. If the Exchequer were not in London, then the Mayor was to present himself at the Tower of London to the Constable of the Tower, or to his Lieutenant.

The annual Ridings to Westminster or the Tower of London did not include pageantry, but there was considerable pomp and circumstance about them, clearly designed to impress with their dignity and importance. The Mayor would be accompanied by the beadle of his Company, also on horseback, as were all his fellow Aldermen and other City dignitaries, and the Crafts. The Mayor's minstrels accompanied the procession.

The Sheriffs, too, on these Ridings to Westminster or the Tower were accompanied by minstrels. Music was an integral feature of these occasions. On the death of Henry V, however, when William Walderne was Mayor, the Aldermen and Guilds went with the Mayor to Westminster in barges but without minstrels.

Three pounds nineteen shillings and fourpence is the total sum shown in the Grocers' records as the money spent from June 5, 1427 to July 6, 1428 'for diverse costes and minstrelles atte Shireuis ridyng'. In 1435 the Grocers' Company 'paid be the handys of John Dodyn for mynstrelles . . . amending of Baneris and hire of barges for Thomas Catworthe and Robert Clopton chosen Shireuis, goyny be watir to Westminster.'

Barges were decorated with blue cloth on civic occasions, and with red on royal occasions.

Sir John Norman, Mayor of London in 1453, elected to go by water to Westminster. He was the first Draper to be mayor of London, and Sir John saw to it that honour was done to the occasion. 'A stately barge was built at his private expense, and the Companies imitated his example,' a fact that has been recorded by several contemporary records.

Minstrels accompanied the Mayor when he went by water to Westminster in 1481. The Sheriffs likewise were accompanied by minstrels or trumpeters 'wearing crimson or red hats, and headed by their marshal, in the Company's barge, which would be decorated with banners, pennons and streamers, fringed with silk and beaten with gold.'

It was during those annual water processions to Westminster that came to a head the vexed question concerning the Merchant Taylors' and the Skinners', as to which was the senior Company. It was in the year 1483, as recorded by Humpherus, that the ultimate incident between the two Companies took place. 'From the commencement of the mayor's procession by water, the question whether the Merchant Tailors' or Skinners' Company should have precedence in the procession had been a matter of dispute; a great feud existed between those companies, one barge always attempting to get before the other barge; this year the rival Companies came to blows which resulted in bloodshed and loss of life. In consequence of this, the matter was referred to the Mayor for arbitration, whereupon he decided that for the future the two guilds should alternatively have precedence, and that each year on approaching Westminster they should lash their two barges together and drink as a toast "The Merchant Tailors and Skinners; Skinners and Merchant Tailors; root and branch, may they flourish forever." '

This Solomon-like judgment was scrupulously adhered to by the two Companies, and though they no longer lash their barges together, they dine each other every year.

It would seem that the title 'Lord Mayor' was first used in the 1540s. It must have been assumed, as there appear to have been no letters patent conferring such a title. However, it was used and accepted in 1553 as shown in the account left by one Henry

Machyn, Citizen and Merchant Taylor, describing the water procession of that year:

'On 29 October, the new Lord Mayor, Sir Thomas White went toward Westmynster, craftes of London in their best levery . . . with trumpets blohyng and the whets [waits] playing . . . a goodly fuyst [a galley with oars and sails] trymmed with banners and guns . . . And then came trumpeters blohyng, and then came those in gownes, and capes and hosse and blue sylke slevys . . . and then came a duiflill [devil] and after that cam all the bachelors all in a leaveray, and skarlett hods; and then cam the pageant of Saint John Baptist gorgeously with goodly speeches; and then cam all the kynges trumpeters blowhyng, and every trumpeter having skarlet capes, and the wetes capes and godly banars, and then the craftes and then the wettes playhyng, and then my lord mayrs offesers, and then my lord mayre.'

When Sir William Harper (Merchant Taylor) was installed Lord Mayor of London in 1561, five harpers played during the procession, and there is an entry to the effect that 21 shillings were 'paid to Mr Morre for the hyer of V harpe and his child playing in the pageant'. There was also a 'grett shutyng of gunnes and trumpettes and blohyng . . . and so to Powlles [St Paul's] chyrche-yarde, and ther met ym a pagantt gorgyously mad, with chylderyn, with dyvers instrumentes playing and syngyng.'

In 1562 the Lord Mayor on his return by water from Westminster was welcomed as he set foot on City soil with 'a goodly pagantt with goodly musyke plahying.'

Many of the processions and pageants through the narrow and crowded City streets were preceded by a class of professionals known as Whifflers. They wore a colourful costume, and brandished very sharp swords. Their purpose was to ensure that the procession had a clear way through the crowd, and this they achieved by waving their swords. This brandishing was done as a form of ceremonial in itself, following various and complicated movements, somewhat after the style of a sword dance.

Such was the professional dexterity of the whifflers that though they appeared to endanger the bystanders, in fact they never hurt anyone. Those flashing, waving swords were quite sufficient for the crowd good-humouredly to draw back. The whifflers, too, had the classic jongleur's skill of being able to throw their swords high in the air and always catch their weapons by the hilt when they fell. The whole effect was dramatic, colourful, and very entertaining. It was also efficient.

There is no doubt that those early pageants and processions – whether they were the Lord Mayor's Show or a Royal Entry – were immensely popular with the citizens and, indeed, formed an important feature of their lives. There was the uninhibited enthusiasm to make the best of life, and such feast days were occasions for rejoicing, in which the City excelled.

When Henry VI came to the City on his return from France, at St Paul's hosts of 'angels' greeted the king with 'divers melodies and songs'.

Then, in the words of the chronicler, 'when he was come to St Paul's, there he alighted down from his horse. And there came the Archbishop of Canterbury and others together with the Dean of St Paul's with his convent, in procession in their best attire of holy church, and met with him, and did him observance . . . and so brought the king to the high altar, with royal song.'

An invariably enthusiastic occasion was the official opening of the Saint Bartholomew's Fair each year. In the year 1604 a Proclamation was issued by the City of London.

'On Saint Bartholomew's Even for the Fair in Smithfield.

'The Aldermen meet my Lord and the Sheriffs at the Guildhall Chapel at two of the Clock after dinner, in their violet gowns lined and their horses, without cloaks, and there hear Evening Prayer; which, being done, they take their horses and ride to Newgate, and so forth to the gate entering in at the Cloth Fair and there make a Proclamation . . .

'Then the Mayor, sheriffs and aldermen, sitting on horseback, robed in their violet gowns, having again made this Proclamation at a point between the City Fair and that owned by the Warwick or Holland family, ride through the Cloth Fair, and return back again, through the churchyard of Great S. Bartholomew's to Aldersgate, and thence home again to the Lord Mayor's house.'

The Proclamation itself was concerned with such matters as keeping the peace and selling wholesome goods. Then, after the trumpets and the pageantry of the mounted procession, comes all the fun of the fair – *The Beggar's Opera*, the plays put on in booths, the music, the roystering, the drinking.

Saint Bartholomew's Fair was one of those seemingly eternal annual features of London life, though even it was to die in the middle of the nineteenth century. Ned Ward writing in his *London Spy* at the end of the seventeenth century describes his experiences there when he listens to a musical programme containing a piece for 'kettledrum and trumpet, performed with such harmonious excellence that no cooper with his asze and driver could have gratified our ears with more delightful music.' Then comes a consort of fiddlers 'with whose melodious diddle-daddle I was so affected that it made my teeth dance in my mouth.' This is followed by a ballad sung in two parts by seven voices, at the conclusion of which Ned Ward calls the lackey who had served him his wine. 'Pray tell our songsters that they deserve to be whipped at the cart's tail for attempting it and that I had rather have an old barber ring Whittington's bells upon a cithern than hear all the music they can make.' Ward philosophically adds: 'Which message I suppose the fellow was afraid to tell 'em, lest they should crack his crown with the bass-fiddle sticks.'

At a slightly later date one Thomas Dale of Aldgate advertised that at his Musick Booth 'you shall be entertained with good Musick, Singing and Dancing, including a Sarabande and a Jig and a young-woman that Dances with fourteen glasses on the Backs and Palms of her Hands and turns round with them above a Hundred times as fast as a Windmill.' At the same booth the customer could regale himself with a variety of drinks while listening to the music and watching the lady spin. He could have wine, beer, mum, syder, ale, and other sorts of liquors. Competition was always keen at Saint Bartholomew's Fair as, according to Ned Ward, 'Music-houses stood thick by another.'

Stow draws the picture of such public occasions in the City of London with vigorous clarity. Thus, in 1618 'On the Vigil of St John Baptist, and on St Peter & Paul the Apostles, every mans dore being shadowed with greene Birch, long Fennell, St John's Wort, Orpin, white Lilies, and such like . . . has also Lamps of glasse, with Oyle burning in them all the night, some hung out branches of Yron curiously wrought, containing hundreds of Lamps lighted at once, which made a good shew, namely in New Fish-street, Thames-street, etc. Then had yee besides the standing watches, all in bright harnesse, in every Ward and street of this Citie and Suburbs, a marching watch, that passed through the principal streets thereof, to wit from the little Conduit by Paules gate, through West Cheape, by the Stocks, through Cornhill, by Leaden Hall to Aldgate, then backe downe Fenchurch streete, by Grasse-church street into Cornehill, and through into West Cheape againe, and so broke up. The whole way orderd for this marching watch extended to 3200 Taylors yards of assize, for the furniture whereof with lights, there were appointed 700 Cressets, 500 of them being found by the Companies, the other 200 by the Chamber of London.

'There were also diuers Pageants, Morris dancers, Constables, . . . The Waytes of the City, . . . The Sheriffes watches came one after the other in like order, but not so large in number as the Maiors: for where the Maior had besides his Giant three Pageants, each of the Sheriffes had besides their Giants but two Pageants, each their Morris Dance and one Henchman.'

During the Midsummer Shows in the City the minstrels were an important feature. No procession was ever complete without the noise of music, whether it was a riding to Westminster, a Royal Entry, or a simple feast day.

When James I made his Royal Entry nine of the St Paul's choir boys, personifying the muses, sang to the accompanyment of viols. The boys sang in an arbour which had been erected near the Little Conduit in Cheap, and was described as The Garden of Plenty. As the King drew near he was hailed from the arbour with the sound of cornets.

It is interesting to know that the King stopped and visited the arbour together with various of the Royal party, where they were entertained with music, and examined the erection and the skill with which it had been constructed. After that the King went on to St Paul's. The choir was ranged on the Cathedral battlements and greeted the King's approach with an anthem. Singing accompanied the procession to Temple Bar.

Charles II was equally musically received. The City was decorated for the Royal Entry, and the Livery Companies, each man wearing his gown and hood, lined the streets from Old Jewry to Temple Bar. Music was provided by the City Waits.

After his Coronation, Charles II on his ride from the Tower to Whitehall was lavishly entertained with music. Thus, there were eight waits stationed on a stage in Crutched Friars, while near Aldgate six waits played from a balcony specially built for the occasion.

More waits were at Leadenhall, while on the top of the conduit at Cornhill there were eight nymphs in white robes, and the King was welcomed with 'a noise of seven trumpets'.

At the Exchange in Cornhill a group of singers dressed as mariners entertained the King with songs, while others played wind-instruments. At the Stocks was a band, the fountain nearby spouted wine and water. The same also flowed from the fountain at Cheap. On the Conduit in Cheap were eight nymphs and eight musicians, and at the Standard six waits.

In fact, there was music the whole way, such was the reception given to Charles II on his Restoration. The City did its best to efface the grim memory of the Civil War on that joyous occasion.

All in all, it is not to be wondered at that England was described on the Continent as 'a nest of singing birds'.

CHAPTER 2

THE CITY WAITS

Written music as we know it today is of fairly recent origin. Tudor music is well recorded in readable form by experts, and the instruments played by musicians of that period are fully understood. When, however, we go back to the music of the twelfth and thirteenth centuries almost all of it has become lost in the muted ages. Written music hardly existed in those days except in a form which was little more than a reminder to those who were already familiar with the tune.

Music of the middle ages, therefore, remains somewhat a matter for conjecture – more so in the case of secular music than of church music, for the monks were at pains to write down the music of their liturgy more thoroughly than was the case with lay musicians.

It is more than likely, too, that the minstrels of those earlier days preferred to keep their music in their own memories – an understandable precaution in the competitive field of popular music.

There are, of course, written records of musical performances as well as artists' drawings of musicians and musical instruments of those early ages, in which the musical airs themselves are lost. The form they took can only be guessed at.

What is certain is that people always danced and sang their songs and listened to the music of others. That is a part of human nature. It is equally certain that twelfth and thirteenth century songs were usually accompanied by a musical instrument such as a small harp.

The form of these accompaniments can only be guessed at, and may well have been impromptu, depending on the skill and mood of the instrumentalist. Early manuscripts only give the voice part.

Contemporary illustrations depict the various instruments in the hands of the players, and both illustrations and writings describe harps, bagpipes, shawms, viols, flutes and trumpets, as well as other antique instruments. The viol was very popular as an accompaniment to songs because it had a wide compass and was well suited to the voice. It could be either plucked with the finger, or bowed.

The professional musician was called a jongleur or minstrel. His repertoire would include all kinds of songs as well as dance music. He would also be something of a juggler and acrobat – hence the term jongleur. When he sang he usually accompanied himself.

In London in the fourteenth century there were several well defined classes of minstrels – as, indeed, there are today! Nor were the different groups always on the friendliest terms with each other. Musicianship can be a hard way of earning a living, and competition in that field has always been keen.

There were the minstrels in the king's service, who wore the king's livery. Many of them lived in the City for a good part of the year at least. Others were of the households of noble families. They and the king's minstrels could be described as the aristocrats of minstrelsy, protected, assured. Then there were those who were granted the right to wear the livery of the King's Musick, but were not actually in the Royal pay. Such minstrels had been examined in their musical skill, and the grant to wear the livery was, in effect, the equivalent to the obtaining of a degree in music. Wherever they went, such minstrels were usually well received and welcomed.

In the City of London there were also the professional minstrels who were freemen, and wore the livery or badge of the guild or fellowship to which they belonged. Being dependent on picking up their livelihood where they could find it, their livery was an undoubted asset at all times, for it gave social status to the wearer, and was a guarantee of integrity.

At the lower end of the scale were the lone minstrels, freelances who drifted from place to place where opportunity seemed most likely. The relatively great population of London and its constant flow of visitors was a certain draw. Such wandering minstrels with their harp and a handful of songs were mostly acquainted with sleight of hand, acrobatics, and tumbling and juggling as sidelines to their minstrelsy. These interlopers to London were, so to speak, gate-crashers in the City, and were credited with being not over-particular as to how they obtained the wherewithal to scrape a living. The wandering minstrel of romantic legend was, very often, 'the rogue and vagabond and sturdy beggar' against whom the Act of Queen Elizabeth in 1597 was directed, which rendered him liable to punishment when found wandering abroad. It was, therefore, greatly to his advantage to obtain by any means, whether he was entitled to it or not, a livery which consisted of a cloak and badge bearing the arms of the king or of a nobleman, or of a city, if he were to avoid trouble.

These 'foreign' minstrels, as they were called by the City minstrels, were very much resented by the local minstrels. This resentment was also levelled against the part-time performer. During the day the offender would follow some non-musical trade, but at other times he would turn to that of a musician, which was by no means to the advantage of the full-time professional. Furthermore, the part-time minstrels were generally inferior in their musical skill. The lower grades would play in alehouses and 'pass the hat round'. This lowered the whole tone of the art and science of music.

Action was constantly sought from the Aldermen to prevent part-time musicians from performing in the City. It was a considerable problem, for often the offenders were themselves freemen of other guilds, and as the mere act of playing a musical instrument was not in itself a crime, it was not easy for the authorities to prevent the part-time musician from trying his luck.

Last, but by no means least on the list of musicians in the City were the Waits. There were City Waits when the craftsmen of London were combining together into guilds and brotherhoods. One can find entries in the City Letter Books on this matter in the years 1334, 1337, and 1371, but there is no complete history of their duties as watchmen and as entertainers.

The waits were, in a sense, men apart. They were the City's official musicians, and they were paid a regular, though not large, wage. They had, also, the benefit of a pension at the end of their working life. They were freemen of the City; they wore the livery of the City, which included a valuable silver badge depending from a heavy silver chain that hung about their necks. Their duties were to provide music at City functions, both royal and civic, as well as on festive occasions. They also carried out certain watchman's duties.

Originally, the waits were night watchmen, neither more nor less. Every royal palace, castle, camp, and walled town had its waits. Their duties were various, and included calling the hours of the night so that the guards might be changed at their due times. As they made their rounds they reported in strident tones the state of the weather ('Past three o'clock and a cold frosty morning'), and were on the alert for any sign of fire. They kept a look-out for strangers and suspicious happenings, and were ready to sound an alarm with an ox-horn or its metal equivalent.

Their origins lay in the twelfth and thirteenth centuries when the cities obtained the right of self-government, the right to fortify their town, and, because the times were lawless, the right to create military forces for defence of property.

Curiously enough, it was the loud and most unmusical instrument, the ox-horn, that in the course of time turned the watchmen into musicians. As musical instruments improved so the waits were provided with better instruments. In place of the ox-horn came the shawm, which was a primitive oboe. There were also wooden cornets and sackbuts. Other instruments followed of increasing sophistication, and, having time on their hands, the musical skill of the waits kept pace with the instruments provided. With this added skill their duties widened. Thus, persons of importance were awakened by the playing of soft music at their doors.

In *The History of the Worshipful Company of Musicians of London* it is shown that the word 'wait' can be traced through various Teutonic dialects. For example, the Gothic and Icelandic 'waca' and the Anglo-Saxon 'wacian' signify to wake, to watch, to guard. There is also the old German forms of 'wahta' or 'wahte', and the modern German 'wachter', all meaning to watch or guard.

Henry III (1216–1274) first established waits in London. According to Stow this was in the year 1253. In 1296 it was enacted that each gate of the City of London shall be 'shut by the servant dwelling there, and that he shall have a wayt at his own expense.'

By the fifteenth century London and other important towns were becoming the principal employers of waits. They had attained a state in which they were primarily musicians, and the duties of watchmen were only secondary. Except for the minstrels of the King's Musick, they were the official makers of secular music in the City.

Their number on the City pay-roll varied from time to time. From 1475 until 1650 the Court of Aldermen considered six waits to be the proper number, though with their trained apprentices their effective strength was often more. In later years they were increased to eighteen or twenty.

The records show that in 1526 the City Corporation bought the waits a sackbut to augment the shawms with which they were then equipped. Further sackbuts were added in 1555 and 1559.

Sackbuts were an early form of trombone. The waits also included cornets in their repertoire of instruments.

They were by now the City's official musicians, with a continually increasing range of musical instruments at their disposal. Their ability as musicians must have been considerable. Thomas Morley published his *Consort Lessons* in 1599, and dedicated the work to the Lord Mayor and Aldermen, and in his dedication highly praised the skill of the City Waits. The *Lessons* were mainly for stringed instruments – the treble lute, pandora, cittern and bass viol – but also for the flute and treble flute.

Morley himself was organist at St Paul's Cathedral, and for some years held the monopoly of music-printing in London – a monopoly granted him by Queen Elizabeth.

The Records of the Court of Aldermen itemise each musical instrument bought for the waits from time to time. For example:

1569, 'The Waits to be paid for a set of Recorders and six Cornets.'

1576, 'Certain new instruments.'

1581, 'Two more sackbuts.'

1597, 'The Chamberlain shall presently buy and provide several instruments called a double saggbutt, a single saggbut, and a curtal [like a bassoon] for the musicians at the charge of the City.'

By the end of the sixteenth century the waits had at their disposal a wide range of instruments, and their skill in playing in consort had become famous. In addition to the traditional wait-pipes or shawms, curtal, recorders, cornets and sackbuts, as representing the wind instruments, they also played on viols, harps and lutes, as well as several keyboard instruments such as the portable organ.

Their official position in the City was naturally an enviable one. If a vacancy occurred there were always minstrels eager to fill it, offering themselves for examination to show that they were skilled enough to be worthy of the appointment.

The waits were the musicians in attendance upon the Lord

Mayor and Sheriffs, and they performed at both official and private functions. They had their marching duties in which they took part as musicians in processions and the like. They also played at official and private functions. During the night hours they were the City Watchmen. Thus their role was divided between protection and entertainment.

Though the waits were not well paid, to our way of thinking, there were many 'perks' to be found. In their free time they could accept outside engagements for which they received remuneration that was often higher than their regular wages.

In addition to playing musical instruments, the waits added singing to their accomplishments. Henry Machyn wrote in his diary in 1555:

'A goodly procession from St Peter's in Cornhill with the fishmongers, and my Lord Mayor, with a hundred copes, unto Paul's, and there they offered; with the waits playing and singing.'

In the early years of the seventeenth century the waits' singing was termed 'the City music of voices', which speaks highly of their performance. To augment the waits, men skilled in singing were employed by the Corporation as extras. A boy 'that shall have a special good voice in singing' was taken on as an apprentice by the waits. Later, two other boys were likewise apprenticed for their singing.

Then in the year 1613 a lute player with a fine singing voice was appointed to the waits. In every possible way 'the City music of voices' was nurtured by the Aldermen, so that in time a highly competent choir of waits was established – men with trained voices able to accompany themselves on lutes and such lute-like instruments as the orpharion and poliphon, and the bass viol. Boys' voices and men's voices sang in complete consort.

Truly the waits had moved a long way from the early watchmen's days with ox-horn and shawm. In fact, the watchman's side of the duties had become so relatively unimportant that when a wait sought to resign from his service because he was 'not able to watch in the night season', rather than let so able a musician go, the Aldermen let him off the watch duties. The Corporation no doubt found a substitute to do the night watches, which were still important in themselves. Thus, it is recorded that in 1634 a wait for medical reasons was given permission to provide a substitute to do the night watches for him.

To have produced so fine a result musically, the waits must have been a well-disciplined group. The pay they received for it, however, was never very high. Thus, in 1475 the annual payment per wait was £1 6s. 8d. In 1524 it was increased to £3 6s. 8d. In 1536 wages went up to £6 a year per man. Between the years 1568 and 1582 yearly wages rose from £8 to £11 13s. 4d. During James I's reign it leapt to £20.

The waits first received their distinctive livery and clothing in 1442. In addition to his blue gown and red cap, each wait wore his silver collar of SS,* from which depended a silver badge bearing the Arms of the City. The collar and badge together weighed about 13 ounces, and in the year 1582 were valued at £3 7s. 6d.

One wait lost his silver collar and badge, and was made to pay for it out of his wages. Another pawned his, and it was never redeemed. The wait died and the City had to bear the loss. After that no chances were taken. All waits who did not own their badges (some did) had to find security for them, and until that security was forthcoming wages were withheld.

The waits played an important part in the old marching watches which were something between a Lord Mayor's Procession and a military review. Their position was near the head of the procession, immediately behind the Lord Mayor's party. The waits were followed by the 'other city officials, grave persons, ensigns, players, morris dancers, twenty-five drums, thirteen fifes, and two or more groups of musicians.'

When Sir William Harper went to Westminster in 1561, in

* *Spiritus Sanctus.* The letters S were entwined.

addition to the five harps, music was provided by the waits, also by trumpets, drum and flutes, regals, and by the children of the choir 'of the late monastery of Westminster'.

In 1575 the Lord Mayor went by water to Westminster. On his return to the City, Lord Mayor and Aldermen mounted their horses and rode along the lines of liverymen in Cheapside. With the touch of saturnalia which so often characterised such shows, the procession was led by devils and others fantastically dressed. There were also whifflers in velvet coats, and wearing chains of gold, who were armed with staves to keep the way clear. There were trumpeters, the drum and flute of the city, and seventy of so poor men in blue gowns with red sleeves, and armed with pikes and targets. The City waits were also in their blue gowns with red sleeves and caps. They, however, were distinguished in their livery from that of the poor men by the silver collars and silver badges they wore.

Regarding the touch of saturnalia occurring in the City ceremonials, the irrepressible Ned Ward, London Tavern Keeper and Humorous writer, writing about 125 years later, touched on the subject in the *London Spy*.

'We heard a Noise so dreadful and surprising, that we thought the Devil was Riding or Hunting through the City.

'At last bolted out from the Corner of a Street, with an *Ignis Fatus* Dancing before them, a parcel of strange *Hobgoblins* cover'd with long Frize Rugs and Blankets, hoop'd round with Leather Girdles . . . and their Noddles button'd up into Caps of martial Figure, like a *Knight Errant* at Tilt and Turnament, with his Wooden-Head lock't in an Iron Helmet; one Armed, as I thought, with a lusty Faggot-Bat, and the rest with strange Wooden Weapons in their hands in the shape of Clyster-pipes, but as long, almost as *Speaking-Trumpets*. Of a sudden they clap't them to their Mouths, and made such a frightful Yelling, that I thought the World had been dissolving, and the Terrible Sound of the last Trumpet to be within an inch of my Ears.

'Under these amazing apprehensions, I ask'd my Friend what was the meaning of this Infernal Outcry? Prithee, says he, what's the matter with thee? Thou look'st as if thou wert Gally'd; why these are the City Waits . . . the Topping Tooters of the Town; and have *Gowns, Silver-Chains and Sallaries*, for playing *Lilla Bolaro* to my *Lord Mayor's Horse* through the City.'

CHAPTER 3

MINSTRELS IN THE CITY

'The Minstrels,' wrote Bishop Percy in his *Reliques of Ancient Poetry*, 'were an order of men in the middle ages who subsisted by the arts of poetry and music, and sang to the harp verses composed by themselves, or others.'

The art and practice of minstrelsy is one of importance in both the history of England and the history of London, and the impact of the jongleurs and minstrels can be traced from ancient days to modern times. Always the breed of minstrels have been conspicuous and picturesque; their art has been exercised in all parts of Europe.

The social state of a minstrel ranged from the wandering street performer to that of the privileged principal entertainer at Court, some of whom became the companions and confidants of kings.

When William the Conqueror launched his invasion of England, close at his side was the warrior-minstrel Taillefer, who had always accompanied William in his battles. Taillefer sought and obtained permission from William to strike the first blow against the English and, at the Battle of Hastings, he advanced at the head of the Normans singing of the exploits of Charlemagne and Roland. Repeatedly, with a jongleur's skill, he threw his sword high in the air, catching it by the hilt each time until he fell to an English arrow.

Rahere, who died in 1144, was musician and jongleur to King Henry I, and is venerated as the founder of St Bartholomew's

Hospital in the City of London. Rahere founded the hospital when he renounced secular music and became a monk. That he had been a man in the highest ranks of minstrelsy is evident in that of his own munificence he was able to bestow such a gift.

Richard Coeur de Lion, Richard I of England, is an example of a man of royal blood and a warrior who was also a minstrel. In the days of chivalry there were many of this kind. Richard was esteemed as a Trouvère, an order of aristocratic minstrels of the twelfth and thirteenth centuries, from the northern regions of France.

The Trouvères were of similar quality to the Troubadours of Provence in the south. The Troubadours pre-dated the Trouvères by about one hundred years, but with both orders of minstrels, as with their German imitators, the Minnesingers, the songs they composed and sang were on the theme of praise of women and courtly love. Troubadours and Trouvères achieved the greatest refinements in the art of minstrelsy. The high quality of verse they wrote greatly influenced that of the English, as was evidenced by Chaucer's verse. Chivalry was their inspiration, and with the decay of chivalry so their inspiration declined.

When Richard I was prisoner in an Austrian castle, held by Henry VI of Austria, his friend and fellow Trouvère, Blondel, if legend be true, sought the English King's whereabouts in the guise of his minstrel role. The story has it that Blondel, who is believed to have been Jehan I, Lord of Nestles and chasterlain of Brughes, in his search for the imprisoned Richard used the device of singing songs known only to fellow Trouvères, and that, when outside the wall of the castle in which the King was confined, the Trouvère song that Blondel sang was taken up by the unseen prisoner, and thereby the King was located.

England itself has no long tradition of minstrelsy comparable to that of the Trouvères and Troubadours, and the Norman kings of England, and the later Plantagenets, inclined always to the songs of France. French wines and French chansons were the choice of the Court, which put English songs and English composers into an unfashionable category. It was not until the end of the Wars of the Roses, which had virtually wiped out the old Norman-French aristocracy in England, and brought in the Tudors, that French songs were replaced by English.

While the minstrels were still making songs on the French pattern, the English songs of the common people were being passed from mouth to mouth, many of which have survived to the present day in the form of folk-songs.

A unique example of early English polyphonic music, written in about the year 1240 is the sublime 'round', *Sumer is icumin in.*

The words were written in both English and Latin. This verbal duality is an outstanding and significant instance of a man of education not only producing a musical piece greatly in advance of its time, but with a language break-through as well. The use of English went against all convention, and was to reach its fine fulfilment in the writings of Geoffrey Chaucer.

Sumer is icumin in was a song that went straight to the hearts of the common people with its promise of the cheerful warmth of the strengthening sunlight, the coming of spring and growing seed, the drowsy repetitive call of the cuckoo; 'Lhude sing cuccu!' Its appeal must have been immediate to those ordinary people whose comforts were so much dependent on the weather and season of the year, and whose pleasures at all times could only be of the simplest. Truly a song that would make welcome the English minstrel that sang it.

The minstrels' songs of the twelfth and thirteenth centuries were generally accompanied by the harp or viol – particularly the viol, which accommodated itself so well to the range of the human voice.

Other instruments popular in the repertoire of the minstrels were shawms, trumpets, flutes and bagpipes.

It was in the fourteenth century that the craftsmen of London began to combine together to form trade guilds and associations and fraternities for the purpose of protecting their professional interests. In time the City minstrels followed suit, for they, too, had their business problems in their own precarious occupation. Any system of co-operation which might increase the minstrels security of livelihood was to be desired.

Not the least of their problems was that of competition by 'foreign' musicians – minstrels from outside London who had been attracted to the City – as well as competition from those who followed a different trade, but in their spare time performed in the City taverns, inns, alehouses, and at wedding feasts. In an attempt to prevent overcrowding, the regular minstrels of the City strictly limited the number of their own apprentices.

In the year 1469 Edward IV granted a Charter of Incorporation to the Fraternity of Minstrels of England. The preamble to the Charter speaks of 'the brothers and sisters of the Fraternity of Minstrels of our kingdom in times past formed, established and ordained.' From other evidence it would seem that the reference particularly relates to the minstrels of the City of London, who were not of the King's service, but wore the livery of the City.

The minstrels of the City did not form a Fellowship of their own in the fourteenth century. This is probably explained by the fact that the minstrels were already represented by an influential coterie known as 'The King's Minstrels' or 'The King's Musick'. An entry in the City Letter Book of 1337 points to this by referring to 'The Minstrels and Palfreymen of our Lord the King'.

The Incorporation of the Edward IV Fraternity of Minstrels of England could not, of course, confer upon the Minstrels of the City of London the protection from outside competition which they sought. In that matter they would have to look after their own interests. London with its thronged streets and constant visitors would attract all and sundry who strummed and sang. 'Foreign' minstrels came from all parts, while the ability of the City authorities to help its own native musicians progressively declined as the population of the City spread beyond its walls.

On June 4, 1500, in the fifteenth year of the reign of Henry VII, the City minstrels broke away from the King's Minstrels and founded a fellowship of their own, thereby falling into line with City tradition. They petitioned the Lord Mayor and the Court of Aldermen to grant them Articles of Incorporation for the redress of the old grievance concerning 'foreign' musicians.

In this way was brought into being the Fellowship of Minstrels of the City of London, which conferred upon them the right to see that no person not a freeman of London 'no manner foreyner of whatsoever condition he be of . . . perform minstrelsy or sing or play an instrument, on several of the most profitable occasions.'

The City Minstrels were careful, however, to exempt the King's Minstrels, the Queen's, the Prince's, the King's Mother's, and the minstrels of the Lords of Parliament, who could continue to perform 'the feat of minstrelsy' in the City, so long as they did not live permanently in the City. In the latter case, they would have to join the Fellowship of the City Minstrels.

In this manner the precursor of the present Worshipful Company of Musicians of London came into being, and by this important move the City Minstrels hoped to be able to take effective measures to protect their own interests within the City of London.

In the *History of the Worshipful Company of Musicians*, by H. A. F. Crewdson, occurs the following observation:

'Thus arose a new Guild of Minstrels strong enough to flout the authority, such as it was, of the Chartered Musicians and we may sense the beginnings of the feud, which had such dire consequences for the City Company a hundred and fifty years later.

'The London Guild, however, for the present made no claim to exercise any authority outside the City and its franchises, to which the powers conferred by the Act of Common Council were limited. For the time being there was no conflict with the Chartered Guild on that score and as there were other Guilds of

Minstrels in some of the provincial towns, which probably carried on undisturbed by the King's Minstrels, at first it may not have seemed to the latter that any very serious threat to their authority was offered by the formation of an interior Guild in London.'

Nevertheless, in 1521 the King's Musicians protested to the Aldermen that the existence of the City Fellowship impinged upon the rights of their fraternity.

Undoubtedly the 1500 Ordinance was concerned only with protecting the livelihood of the City Minstrels within their own walls and liberties. The preamble states this fact most clearly. 'The continual recourse of foreign minstrels daily resorting to this City out of all countries of England and enjoying more freedom than the freemen, cause the Minstrels of the City to be brought to such poverty and decay that they are not able to pay "lot and scot" and do their duty as other freemen do, since their living is taken from them by these foreigners.'

The 'foreign' minstrels are accused, to quote again from the Musicians' Company's *History*, 'of outrageous behaviour and of annoying the good citizens by pressing to their tables at Church Holidays, Weddings and Feasts . . . Uninvited, sometimes as many as five or six at a time crowd to the end of the tables, playing without skill and causing great pain and displeasure to the Citizens and to their honest friends and neighbours.'

Two years after the incorporation of the City Minstrels there was a petition by the City Waits for assistance from the Court of Aldermen. Their plea and complaint was that 'whereas it had "from time out of mind" been customary by virtue of their employment that the Waits should be admitted Freemen of the City, the Fellowship of Minstrels were now demanding that the Waits should not be allowed "to occupy and buy and sell" within the City unless they had been admitted Freemen of the City in the Craft of Minstrels, but that they were too poor to buy their Freedom through the Craft. They, therefore, prayed that they might be admitted to the Freedom in the Guild without payment.'

It would appear, however, that those Waits who had obtained their freedom of the City through Companies other than the Musicians were exempt. As an example of this, Clement Newthe, Citizen and Cordwainer was made City Fife in 1673. The demand, therefore, applied only to those waits who were not already freemen of one or another of the Companies, and that they should obtain their Freedom through the Musicians' Guild without fine.

In 1554 the Musicians petitioned the Court of Aldermen for a new Act. This was because of the persistent competition within the City boundaries, which was growing more acute each year and endangering the livelihood of the honest minstrels.

The new Act was passed and was mainly directed against 'foreigners', who it was claimed were still causing great loss and 'Hindraunce of the gaines and profits of the poore Minstrels being freemen of the Cytie.' Once more the 'foreigners' were forbidden to sing or play on instruments 'in any common hall, tavern, inn, alehouse', or any like place within the City upon pain first of admonition by the Master and Wardens, and then for subsequent offences a fine of 3s. 4d. on each occasion. Half of such fines were to be paid for the use of the 'poore infants in Crysts hospytall and half to the Guild'.

The Act also reimposed the restriction upon the minstrels of the City not to take more than one Apprentice at a time, to avoid overcrowding the profession. Then followed certain new rules:

1. It is an offence to play upon any instrument within the City or liberties of the same in open Streets Lanes or Alleys thereof after ten o'clock in the evening until five o'clock in the morning. (This rule, however, was not to apply to the waits playing or keeping their accustomed watch.)

2. Because many Artificers and Handicraftsmen such as a 'Tayllers, shoemakers and such others', singing songs 'called Three Mens Songs in the Taverns, innes and such other places in this Cytie, and also at weddings to the great loss of the poor

fellowship of minstrels' it is enacted that such conduct is to cease under penalty for disobedience.

(The term 'Three Mens Songs' relates to a form of song in three parts, calling for that number of singers. They were also sometimes referred to as 'Freemen's Songs'.)

3. No minstrel either foreign or freeman or any other person is to keep or teach any school of dancing within the City or liberties. The fine for disobedience to this law is £10.

In the middle years of the sixteenth century there were strong and determined attempts on the part of the authorities to stamp out dancing. Queen Mary Tudor with her strangely morbid and moody disposition was partly to blame for this condemnation of dancing. Because music usually accompanied dancing, the teachers and keepers of dancing schools were themselves usually musicians. One such dancing master was a tenant at the Pewterers' Hall. At the beginning of Mary's reign the Court of Aldermen refused to permit two minstrels to keep a dancing school. Much of the work of suppressing dancing devolved on the Musicians' Company.

In the year 1555 the Lord Mayor by Command of the Queen directed the Court of Aldermen to see that there were no dancing halls in the City or liberties. Each Alderman was called upon to assemble before him all the keepers of taverns, dancing houses and the like in his Ward, and direct them not to permit 'any minstrel or minstrels or any other whatsoever person or persons to sing any manner of song or songs or play upon any manner of instrument to make or play any manner of interlude or play within his or their house.' An exception was made only for marriages and similar festivities.

But minstrels and dancing teachers were not so easily discouraged. In 1562, four years after Elizabeth had ascended the throne and times had mellowed, the Lord Mayor called before him all the minstrels and dancing teachers practising in the City to admonish them to be obedient to the Master and Wardens of the Fellowship of Minstrels.

By the year 1574 the City Corporation's official attitude towards dancing schools within the City bounds had relaxed even further. A committee was appointed to allow or disallow as many of the Company of Minstrels as it decided 'were meet and expedient to keep dancing schools within this City'.

In 1604, the first year of the reign of James I, the City musicians were authorised to control all teachers of dancing. The teachers themselves were required to be citizens of the City but not necessarily freemen of the Company. The Company were instructed to forbid any to teach who were not well qualified. The by-laws also forbade teachers of dancing, licensed or otherwise, and all musicians, 'to teach, keep, or play, haunt, exercise, or use, any dancing in any school of dancing upon any Sabbath days,' upon pain of a fine of £2 for each offence.

Despite the restrictions on the practice of their profession, things had so far gone well enough with the Fellowship of Minstrels. They were very largely masters of their own affairs. Then in the year 1604 the City Minstrels made a move which was later to bring them a great deal of trouble and loss of prestige.

It came about this way. The Fellowship sought a license from the Court of Aldermen to apply to King James I for a Charter of Incorporation. This was accorded by the Aldermen, and on July 8, 1604 the King granted the Charter to the Society of Minstrels of the City of London.

The title conferred upon them by the Charter was 'Master Wardens and Commonalty of the Art or Science of the Musicians of London'. By its Charter the Company was given the power to make by-laws and Ordinances for the government of the Company and of all Minstrels and Musicians of the City of London and within three miles of the City, and to impose reasonable fines and penalties for breach of the by-laws and ordinances.

The by-laws were confirmed by the Lord Chancellor on August 25, 1606. It included regulations concerning apprentices, permitting only one apprentice at a time, except under certain conditions. A standard of entertainment that conformed with propriety, was required, as follows:

'Neither shall any person sing any ribaldry, wanton or lascivious songs or ditties at any time or place within the City of London or liberties thereof, or within three miles of the same city, whereby God may be dishonoured, or any slander or infamy may arise or be given of or to the said science, upon pain that every person offending against the true meaning of this branch of this said Act shall forfeit for his offence ten shillings, and suffer imprisonment of his or their bodies for such convenient time as shall be thought fit by the discretion of the master and wardens of the same society for the time being.'

It is interesting to observe that some few years later, in 1615, the Aldermen as if not fully trusting the City Musicians in the matter of rigidly guarding public morality, ordered that 'no Latin, Italian or French song whatsoever shall be sung till it be first read in English to the Lord Mayor . . . and by him allowed.'

An item in the by-laws rules that 'it is likewise ordained and established that no person or persons free of the said Art or Science of Musicians, nor any of their servants or apprentices, nor any other person or persons using or exercising the said Art or Science, or any of their apprentices or servants whatsoever, shall play at any weddings, feasts, banquets, revels, or other assemblies or meetings within the City of London, suburb or precincts aforesaid, under the number of four, in consort or with violins, upon pain that the master of every such servant, and apprentice, and for every time he or they shall offend contrary to the ordinance, the sum of three shillings and fourpence.'

It will have been noted that the new Charter granted by King James conferred authority upon the City Company to *within three miles of the City*. This included Westminster, and the unavoidable inference was that it gave the City Musicians Guild authority over the King's Musicians in Westminster. It is hardly surprising that this was resented in no uncertain manner by the King's Minstrels, and in due time when it suited them they reacted vigorously.

There seems no doubt that as time went by the City Company had endeavoured to exclude those musicians and minstrels entered into the King's service from teaching and practising music in London if they would not join the Company or 'purchase its approbation thereto.'

Suddenly a Writ was issued in the Court of Chancery against the City Company, and the case came up in the Hilary Term of 1634. There was no difficulty in demolishing the claims of the City Minstrels. The King's Minstrels cited the Charter of Edward IV which he had granted to 'his own beloved Minstrels.' The King's Minstrels likewise did not fail to draw attention to the fact that originally the King's Minstrels had been the principal members of the Company, and that the Musicians of London had broken away by placing themselves under the direct protection of the Lord Mayor and Aldermen. It had been from the Lord Mayor and not from the Crown that they had obtained their subsequent powers until they obtained the grant of a Charter from King James I.

It was now claimed that the Charter of James I had been obtained by the City Minstrels by fraud because they had not disclosed the earlier Charter of Edward IV.

There could be no reply to this shattering argument, and the unfortunate City Minstrels capitulated. The Charter which had been granted by James I was revoked, and the King's Minstrels, to make quite sure that their position would not again be assailed, obtained a new Charter from Charles I. They were now the sole authority empowered to govern the practice of music in England (excepting the county of Cheshire which had its own Royal Ordinances), but specifically including the City of London.

The new Charter, dated July 15, 1635, is preserved in the Records Office, and it makes harsh reading. It recites the Charter

D   49

of Edward IV, and goes on to state that 'certain persons suggesting themselves to be freemen of a pretended society of minstrells in the cittie of London in prejudice of the liberties and privileges aforesaid in the said recited letters patents mencioned and intended to the minstrelles and musicians of the said King and his heires did by untrue suggestions procure of and from King James of ever blessed memory letters patent under his great seale of England . . . And amongst divers other priviledges to graunt unto them the survey scrutiny correction and government of all and singular musicians and minstrells within the said cittie and within three miles of the same cittie . . . '

The Musicians of the City were now without either Royal or municipal authority to control the profession of music within the jurisdiction of the City. But they were resilient in defeat, and lost no time in repairing their loss as best they could, reorganising their shattered forces under the title of 'Master, Wardens and Commonalty of Minstrels, London'.

Three years later, in 1638, the Court of Aldermen recognised them as 'an Ancient Brotherhood of this Cittie, governed by the acts and orders of this honourable Court,' and granted them a new constitutional ordinance.

With specific intent, so as to emphasise the antiquity of the Minstrels' Fellowship, and clearly with the view to anticipating and stifling any possible suggestion that the creation of the City Minstrels' Fellowship was illegal by being contrary to the monopoly of the Royal Charter, the Court of Aldermen made the new ordinance largely a restatement of the 1500 Charter, which had explicitly given the City Company the authority to forbid every person not a freeman of London to 'perform minstrelsy, or sing or play on an instrument, on several of the most profitable occasions . . . '

The aftermath of the war between the Minstrels of the City and the Royal Musicians hardly went according to expectations, though in March 1637 the Westminster Company was claiming authority over the City minstrels, who promptly sought protection from the Aldermen.

It is to be noted with some surprise that despite their brand new Charter of Incorporation from Charles I, which made them the sole authority empowered to govern the practice of music in all England (except Cheshire), the Royal Musicians did not meet again until 1661, twenty-six years later!

The disturbed situation in the country somewhat accounted for this. Seven years after the date of the new Charter war broke out between King and Parliament, which for a while totally eclipsed the King's Musick. (It also nearly eclipsed the City waits, whose pay was stopped at the start of the Civil War. In 1644 seven waits petitioned the Corporation on the matter, stating their poverty. The Aldermen then ordered a resumption of payment of the waits' wages).

When Charles II was restored to the throne the King's Musicians applied for confirmation of their Charter, which the King immediately granted them. The quarrel between the two bodies of minstrels was revived, and the Westminster Company took out a writ of Quo Warranto against them. That was in 1665. The City Minstrels immediately petitioned the Court of Aldermen, stating that they had been put to great trouble and expense in consequence of his Majesty's Musicians' persecution of them for exercising the art and privilege of their Company within the City and liberties. And now the King's Musicians had issued a Quo Warranto against them, seeking wholly to destroy their Society and Government, and to subject them to their own rule and authority.

How this quarrel fared is not known. There is no record of it to be found in the Minute Book. Records, anyway, tended to become obscured in consequence of the Great Plague of London, and the subsequent Great Fire. Certain it is, however, that the City Minstrels Company was still in being in the City in 1677.

In that year the records show that they were directed by the

Court of Aldermen to see to the implementing of an Order of the Court that no musician (except the Common Waits of the City) should play upon Instruments in the open streets in the night time after 10 p.m. and before 5 a.m., and that no person not being a freeman of the City should sing or play in any Common Hall, Tavern, Alehouse, or other like place.

It is quite evident that some of the fire had gone out of the musicians at Westminster. Several of their more militant members of other days were dead. The Minute Book from 1661 to 1679 shows some attempt to exercise their powers, and then the entries cease. The last Minuted meeting is dated July 2, 1678, and thereafter, it would seem, the Westminster Guild became extinct.

In 1763 an action was successfully fought before the Recorder of London by the City Musicians against a man called Hudson, who had employed as musicians at a Lord Mayor's banquet persons not 'free of the Company'. The Guild's position was now a strong one, and it extended to teachers of dancing who, if they were not members of the Guild, could be fined £4 if they dared to give dancing lessons within the City.

Gradually the word 'Minstrel' gave place to 'Musician' which latter word is used by the present day Worshipful Company of Musicians of London. The Charter that they so unhappily lost when it was revoked by Charles I was replaced in 1950 when George VI granted the Company a new Charter on December 29.

The City Waits did not survive. Nineteenth century education and the spread of musical art and appreciation made the waits an anachronism in a rapidly changing world. In their day they had claimed notable members. There was John Ravenscroft, a Wait of Tower Hamlets, who wrote many hornpipe tunes. He died in 1745. Then there was John Banister, who was born in 1630, and was the son and pupil of a St Giles' wait. He was a violinist and became the leader of the band of Charles I.

The death knell of the waits of London came in 1833.

'The Swordbearer recommends the Waits to the Court of

Aldermen, who appoint and admit them. We believe that these offices were in former times held by musicians of high repute in the country, but they have now become utterly insignificant. There were formerly eight of these officers; now there are but three, and vacancies will probably not be filled up. We cannot learn that the City Waits have at present any functions or privileges. We believe that formerly the right of performing for hire in musical entertainments in the City was confined to the Waits. In 1833 the Waits received £5 13s. 4d. each for salary, and £2 16s. for livery.'

And in this manner the once famous Waits of the City of London were allowed quietly to fade away.

CHAPTER 4

THE LONDON CRYES

'There is nothing which more astonishes a foreigner and frightens a country 'squire, than the *cries of London.*'

Thus observed Joseph Addison (1672–1719), poet and essayist, in one of the pieces he wrote for *The Spectator.* The incisive pen draws a satirical echo and picture of the sounds and the streets of seventeenth-eighteenth century London that are as lively as the cries they describe.

'The cries of London may be divided into vocal and instrumental. A freeman of London has the privilege of disturbing a whole street for an hour together with the twankling of a brass kettle or a frying-pan. The watchman's thump at midnight startles us in our beds, as much as the breaking in of a thief. The sow-gelder's horn has indeed something musical in it, but this is seldom heard within the liberties. . . .

'Vocal cries are of a much larger extent, and indeed so full of incongruities and barbarism, that we appear a distracted city to foreigners, who do not comprehend the meaning of such enormous outcries. Milk is generally sold in a note above *Ela*, and it sounds so exceedingly shrill, that it often sets our teeth on edge. The chimney-sweeper is confined to no certain pitch; he sometimes utters himself in the deepest bass, and sometimes in the sharpest treble. . . . The same observation might be made on the retailers of small coal, not to mention broken glasses or brick-dust. . . .

'An honest splenetic gentleman of my acquaintance bargained

with one of them never to come into the street where he lived; but what was the effect of this contract? Why, the whole tribe of card-matchmakers which frequent that quarter, passed by his door the very next day, in hopes of being bought off after the same manner. . . .

'Nor must I omit those excessive alarms with which several boisterous rustics infest our streets in turnip-season; and which are more inexcusable, because those are wares which are in no danger of cooling upon their hands.

'There are others who effect a very slow time, and are, in my opinion, much more trouble than the former; the cooper in particular swells his last note in a hollow voice, that is not without its harmony; nor can I forbear being inspired with a most agreeable melancholy, when I hear that sad and solemn air with which the public are very often asked, If they have any chairs to mend? Your own memory may suggest to you many other lamentable ditties of the same nature, in which music is wonderfully languishing and melodious.

'I am always pleased with that particular time of the year which is proper for the pickling of dill and cucumbers; but alas! this cry, like the cry of the nightingale, is not heard above two months. It would therefore be worth while to consider, whether the same air might not in some cases be adapted to other words.

'It might likewise deserve our most serious consideration, how far, in a well-regulated city, those humourists are to be tolerated, who, not content with the traditional cries of their forefathers, have invented particular songs and tunes of their own: such as was not many years since, the pastry-man, commonly known by the name of the Colly-Molly-Puff. . . .

'I must not here omit one particular absurdity which runs through this whole vociferous generation, and which renders their cries very often not only incommodious, but altogether useless to the public; I mean that idle accomplishment which they all of them aim at, of crying so as not to be understood . . . I have sometimes seen a country boy run out to buy apples of a bellows-mender, and ginger-bread from a grinder of knives and scissors.'

Granting Addison's own entertaining brand of cynicism, the old cries of London were altogether a practical means for selling wares and skills, as noisy and demanding as are the cries of the stallholders in Petticoat Lane on a Sunday morning. Each cry was distinctive, the series of notes recognisable even if the words were not, and the longer versions, in the form of tradesmen's songs, had their own familiar tunes.

A Benedictine monk whose name was Dan John Lydgate, born 1370 and died 1450, a friend of Chaucer, and a prolific writer, has given us the earliest record of the words of the cries of London. The poem is entitled *London Lackpenny*, which tells the story of a man from Kent who went to London to seek legal redress in the matter of some goods of which he had been defrauded.

The unfortunate man is almost penniless, and in consequence he receives very little shrift from the lawyers. At last he decides to make his way home. In Westminster his hood is stolen, and as he passes through the City he sees it hung up for sale in Cornhill 'where was much stolen gear among.'

London Lackpenny is a remarkable work, and its imagery of fifteenth century London brilliantly clear:

'Then unto London I did me hie,
　　Of all the land it beareth the prize;
Hot Peascods! one began to cry;
　　Strawberry ripe, and Cherries in the rise!
　　One bade me come near and buy some spice;
Pepper and saffron they gan me *bede;* [offered to me]
But for lack of money, I might not speed.

Then to the Chepe I began me drawn,
　　Where much people I saw for the stand;
One offerene me velvet, silk and lawn;
　　Another he taketh me by the hand,

"Here is Paris thread, the finest in the land."
I never was used to such things indeed;
And, wanting money, I might not speed.

Then went I forth by London Stone,
    Throughout all Canwyke Street:
Drapers much cloth me offered anon;
    Then came in one crying "Hot Sheep's feet";
    One cried mackerel, rushes green, another gan greet;
One bad me buy a hood to cover my head;
But for the want of money, I might not speed.

Then I hied me into East-chepe,
    One cries ribs of beef, and many a pie;
Pewter pots they clattered on a heap;
    There was harp, pipe, and minstrelsy;
    "Yes by Cock! Nay by Cock!" some began cry;
Some sung of Jenkin and Julian for their mead;
But for lack of money, I might not speed.

Then into Cornhill anon I *yode*, [went]
    Where was much stolen gear among;
I saw where hung mine own hood
    That I had lost among the throng;
    To buy my own hood I thought it wrong;
I knew it well, as I did my creed;
But, for lack of money, I could not speed.

The taverner took me by the sleeve,
    "Sir," saith he, "will you our wine assay?"
I answered "That cannot be much grieve,
    A penny can do more than it may";
    I drank a pint, and for it did pay;
Yet, sore a-hungered from hence I yode,
And, wanting money, I could not speed.'

The Canwyke Street of Lydgate's London is the Cannon Street

of today. The din of the great City thoroughfares of a London of more than five hundred years ago with the shouts and cries of the itinerant retailers and pedlars spoke the brisk music of trade which has always been the City's keynote.

In a comedy called *Three Ladies of London*, printed in 1584 by Roger Warde, 'dwelling neere Holburne Conduit at the sign of the Talbot,' is to be found the following poetical rendering of various London cries of the time.

> 'New broomes, green broomes, will you buy any?
> Come maydens, come quickly, let me take a penny.
> > My broomes are not steeped
> > But very well bound:
> > My broomes be not crooked,
> > But smooth cut and round.
> > I wish it would please you,
> > To buy of my broome:
> > Then would it well ease me,
> > If market were done.
> > Have you any olde bootes,
> > Or any olde shoone:
> > Powch-ringes, or buskins,
> > To cope for new broome?
> > If so you have, maydens,
> > I pray you bring hither;
> > That you and I, friendly,
> > May bargain together.
> New broomes, green broomes, will you buy any?
> Come maydens, come quickly, let me take a penny.'

Lydgate was invited by the Corporation of the City to record various civic ceremonies in verse. He wrote a 'ballade' to the Aldermen and Sheriffs on May Day, and he devised pageants for both the Mercers' Company and the Goldsmiths' in honour of William Estfield, who was twice Lord Mayor of London – in

1429 and 1437. The Chapter of St Paul's also commissioned Lydgate to write verses to be inscribed beneath a pictorial representation in the Cloisters of the Dance of Death.

The same Benedictine monk who knew his London so well, also wrote a poem describing the military expedition of Henry V to France in 1415, *The Battle of Agincourt*, and the King's reception in London on his triumphant return.

'Into Paules then rode our King,
XIII Bysshops heir mette them right,
The greate Belles thann did they ring,
Upon his feet full faire he light
And to the high Altar he went right.
To Deum for Joye thann they gan sing
And then he offered to God Almyght,
And then to Westminster he went without dwellying,
Gloria Tibi Trinitas.'

Rather surprisingly, among the cacophony of sound that went to make up the noise of music in London the bagpipes were a familiar feature. Sir John Dalyell, in his *Musical Memoirs of Scotland*, which he wrote in about 1849, observes that 'The bagpipe occupies more frequent notice in England than in Scottish history and is a more frequent object both of delineation and sculpture.' Henry VIII had his 'baggepiper', and he left in his collection of musical instruments four 'with pipes of ivorie'.

Lydgate's friend Geoffrey Chaucer in his *Canterbury Tales* takes his pilgrims out of town to the music of the Miller's pipe. From contemporary records the pipes seem to have been regarded as a cheerful accompaniment to a long journey on foot. 'I say to thee,' writes an early fifteenth century chronicler, 'that it is right well done that Pylgremys have with them both singers and also pipers, that when one of them that goeth barefoote, striketh his toe upon a stone, and hurtheth hym sore and maketh hym to blede, it is well done that he and his fellow begyn then a Songe, or else take out of his bosome a Baggepipe for to drive away with suche myrthe the hurte of his fellow.'

Concerning the folk music of the old cries of London, not much is to be gleaned from the contemporary historians. The recording of early music, as we know, was in a primitive state, and tunes were mostly transmitted orally. The tunes of the different trades and the wares that were sold in the streets of the City were traditional tunes that had been handed down from father to son, or mother to daughter. If a particular trade died out the tune ceased to be sung in the streets and would be forgotten.

It is only within living memory that almost the last of the London cries is heard no more in the streets.

> 'Who will buy my sweet lavender?
> Gathered at the break of day.'

Were it not for the later facility for recording music accurately, plus the more modern interest in music for its own sake apart from its practical utility, that particularly musical and wistful air which used to drift from street to street, would be soon forgotten and for ever lost.

All the old Cries of London might have passed into silence, when so much was lost during the Civil War and the Commonwealth, but for a fortunate event. Three of the best composers of Shakespeare's time, Thomas Weelkes, Orlando Gibbons, and Richard Deering, wrote musical 'fancies', or fantasias, on the theme of the street cries of London. In those Fancies are to be found the tunes of almost every recorded London Cry. According to the *Oxford Companion to Music*, there are 150 different cries represented.

The deeper significance of the three *Fancies* is that wherever any of the cries are duplicated in one or other of the compositions, the words and tunes are always identical, and the same music is always associated with the same cry. Thus, we have three impeccable documents on the folk music of the early London streets.

Richard Deering's Fancy, *What d'ye Lacke?* presents a detailed

picture of a long day in the City streets. It begins with the young
apprentices at their stalls or shops and calling their wares in
competition with each other:

> 'What doe ye lack, doe ye buy, sir, see what ye lack?
> Pins, points, garters, Spanish gloves or silk ribbons?
> 'Will ye buy a very fine cabinet, a fine scarfe or a
> rich girdle and hangers?
> 'See here, madam, fine cobweb lawn, good
> cambrick or faire bone lace.
> 'Will ye buy any very fine silk stocks, sir?
> 'See here a faire hat of the French block, sir.'

The apprentices are followed by the fishwives:

> 'Sprats, sprats, sprats!
> Twopence a peck, twopence a peck, twopence a peck,
> at Milford Stairs.'

The blacking seller comes next, he who humped a barrel of
blacking on his back. He sings a tradesmen's song.

> 'Buy any black, buy any black?
> Here comes one dare boldly crack.
> He carries that upon his back
> Will make old shoes look very black.
> Will ye buy any blacking, maides?'

Then is heard the song of the cooper.

> 'A cooper I am and have been long,
> And cooping is my trade;
> And married I am to as pretty a wench
> As ever God had made.
>   Have ye worke for a cooper?'

The rat-catcher comes along with his own quaint song,
sardonic and full of melody at the same time.

'Rats or Mice,
Ha' ye any rats, mice, pol-cats or weasles?
Or ha' ye any old Sows sick o' the measles?
I can kill them, and I can kill moles,
And I can kill vermin
That creepeth up and creepeth down
And peepeth into holes.'

Then comes the strange pathos of the begging song, supplicating alms for prisoners:

'Pity the poor women for the Lord's sake.
Good men of God, pity the poor women.
Poor and cold and comfortless in the deep dungeons.'

Cries the travelling chiropodist: 'Ha' ye any corns on your feet or toes?' The itinerant dentist speaks of himself as 'Kind Heart', and his quaint song, designed to allay the fears of potential customers, is as follows:

'Touch and goes! Touch and goe!
Ha' ye work for Kind Heart the tooth-drawer?
Touch and goe!'

And so the day, too, goes by, with London Cry following London Cry and tradesman's Song, to come to an end at last with the voice of the City Watchman at midnight: 'Twelve o'clock. Look well to your lock.' . . .

The Fancy of Orlando Gibbons follows the same pattern. The voice of the Watchman on his round sings:

'God give you good morrow, my masters,
Past three o'clock and a faire morning.'

The fish women begin their cries of 'Mussels', followed by the oyster women. Then the ink-seller's song:

'Buy any ink,

Will ye buy any ink?
Very fine writing ink;
Will ye buy any ink and pens?'

After the voice of the Town Cryer is the begging song for the
inmates of Bethlehem Hospital:

'Poor naked Bedlam, Tom's a-cold.
A small cut of thy bacon or a piece of
thy Sow's side, good Bessie.
God almighty bless thy witts.'

The song of the chimney-sweep, in which he affirms that after
he has swept your chimney from bottom to the top 'then shall no
soot fall in your poridge pot', is practical and to the point. It is
also claimed that the air to which it is sung is among the most
melodious in the repertoire of London Cries. The Watchman
concludes the progress of the day:

'Twelve o'clock.
Look well to your locks, your fire, and
your light,
And so, Good-night.'

The Watchman's reference to lights harks back to as early as
1416, when the then Mayor of the City, Sir Henry Barton,
ordered lanthorn and lights 'to be hanged out on the winter
evenings betwixt Allhallows and Candlemas.'

Usually, during the long nights there would be a double watch,
the first from six to midnight, and the second from midnight to
seven in the morning, and one of the watchmen's duties was to
see that the order for lights to be hung outside the houses to
illuminate the dark streets was carried out. For three centuries this
practise was maintained, until the reign of Queen Anne, when the
first public street lighting was instituted in London.

It was because so many householders slept through the watchman's strident cry – or chose to ignore it – as he shuffled through

63

the night streets that a Mayor of London in the reign of Queen Mary ordered the Watchman to be provided with a bell to augment his admonishings. Thus armed, in the course of time he came to be known as the Bellman, and he continued to ring this terrible infliction down to the time of the Commonwealth.

The anomaly of this infuriating disturbance lay in the fact that in the reign of Elizabeth The Statute of the Streets prescribed that 'no man shall blow any horn in the night, or whistle after the hour of nine o'clock in the night under pain of imprisonment.' Also forbidden was the making of any 'sudden outcry in the still of the night, or making any affray, or beating his wife.' But the Bellman's diabolical ringing went on unchecked!

Stow tells us that in Queen Mary's day one watchman of each Ward 'began to go all night with a bell, and at every lane's end, and at every ward's end, gave warning of fire and candle, and to help the poor and pray for the dead.'

In 'A Bellman's Song' are the lines of verse:

> 'Maydens to bed, and cover coal,
> Let the mouse out of her hole,
> Crickets in the chimney sing,
> Whilst the little bell doth ring;
> If fast asleep, who can tell
> When the clapper hits the bell?'

The Bellman exhorted those in the houses to make their lanthorns 'bright and clear'. He also informed them how many hours their candles were supposed to burn and illuminate the street for the safety of honest passers-by.

The bellman of St Sepulchre's had the further macabre duty of awakening the prisoners condemned to die on the following morning with the words:

> 'When St Sepulchre's bell to-morrow tolls
> The Lord above have mercy on your souls.'

Above: The Enraged Musician – Hogarth

Below: The Industrious 'Prentice – Hogarth

Cries of London

(Photo: Guildhall Library)

This set of sixteen Cries of London, published in 1735 from the original plates of 1641–2, corresponds with a set of silver counters dated during the reign of Charles I

In the third of the *Fancies*, by Weelkes, cries are given pertaining to nine kinds of fish for sale, four kinds of pies, and eight kinds of fruit. Then there is 'Have you any work for a Tinker?' followed by 'Bellows to mend', and 'Wood to cleave'. There are also the cries of 'Salt', 'Kitchen stuff', 'Coney skins', 'Whyte cabbages, turnips, parsnips, lettuce and radish.'

The famous Roxburghe Ballad, entitled *The Cries of London* is exuberant in its word-painting of the City streets.

> 'Hark! how the cries in every street
> Make lanes and alleys ring;
> With their goods and ware, both nice and rare,
> All in a pleasant lofty strain;
> Come buy my gudgeons fine and new,
> Old cloaths to change for earthen ware,
> Come taste and try before you buy,
> Here's dainty poplin pears.
> Diddle, diddle, diddle dumplins, oh!
> With walnuts nice and brown
> Let none despise the merry, merry cries
> Of famous London town.'

The history of the London Cries is a history of social changes. Dr Johnson wrote in *The Advertiser* concerning London: 'The attention of the new-comer is generally first struck by the multiplicity of cries that stun him in the streets, and the variety of merchandise and manufactures which the shopkeepers expose on every hand.' Today the shopkeeper has almost entirely banished the itinerant salesman and the working tradesman from the streets, and their cries have gone with them. The stallholders of today in Leather Lane are only a shadow of the multitudes who in times past cried their wares and skills in the City streets.

But the echo of the old London streets is still to be found. From *Deuteromelia: or the Second Part of Pleasant Roundelayes*, printed for

E

Thomas Adams, dwelling in Paul's Churchyard, at the sign of the White Lion, 1609, is to be found this Freeman's Song:

'Who liveth so merry in all this land
As doth the poor widdow that selleth the sand?
And ever shee singeth as I can guesse,
Will you buy any sand, any sand, mistress?
The broom-man maketh his living most sweet,
With carrying of brooms from street to street;
Who would desire a pleasanter thing,
Than all the day long to doe nothing but sing?
The chimney-sweeper all the long day,
He singeth and sweepeth the soote away;
Yet when he comes home altho' he be weary
With his sweet wife he maketh full merry.
Who liveth so merry and maketh such sport
As those that be of the poorest sort?
The poorest sort wheresoever they be,
They gather together by one, two, three.
And every man will spend his penny
What makes such a shot among a great many?'

In his *Hesperides* Herrick introduces a verse of the style of a Bellman's poetry. It speaks of the night watches in the City streets, and one senses the loneliness of the Bellman on his rounds:

'From noise of scare-fires rest ye free,
From murders Benedicite;
From all mischances that may fright
Your pleasing slumbers in the night,
Mercy secure ye all, and keep
The goblin from ye while ye sleep.
Past one o'clock, and almost two,
My masters all, "Good day to you!" '

Then there is the warmth of the Good Friday bun sellers, as the boys with their baskets hurry through the early morning streets, earning money to spend during the holiday:

'One-a-penny, poker; two-a-penny, tongs!
One-a-penny; two-a-penny, hot cross buns,
One-a-penny, two-a-penny, hot cross buns!
If your daughters will not eat them, give them to your sons.
But if you haven't any of those pretty little elves,
You cannot do better than eat them up yourselves;
One-a-penny, two-a-penny, hot cross buns:
                    All hot, hot, hot, all hot.
One-a-penny, two-a-penny, hot cross buns!
Burning hot! smoking hot, r-r-r-roking hot –
One-a-penny, two-a-penny, hot cross buns.'

But what was in other days the living voice of the City is now but a ghostly echo of the past, the tunes they sang to the Cries and Tradesmen's Songs, now orphaned from their purpose.

'I sweep your chimnies clean, O.' 'Buy my flowers, sweet flowers, new-cut flowers.' 'Buy Rosemary! Buy Sweetbriar!' 'Newcastle salmon! Dainty fine salmon!' 'Pears for pies! Come feast your eyes! Ripe pears, of every size, who'll buy?' 'One-a-penny, two-a-penny, hot cross buns!' 'Come take a peep, boys, take a peep! Girls, I've the wonder of the world!' 'Buy my flounders! Fine dabs! All alive, O!' 'Some bread and meat for the poor prisoners; for the Lord's sake, pity the Poor!'

The ringing bell of the muffin man can still be remembered by a few, as is the sweetly plaintive 'Who will buy my sweet lavender? Gathered at the break of day.' But the music of the London Cries has been stilled.

CHAPTER 5

ORGANS IN THE CITY

In the City records, dated August 29, 1531, occurs the following:

'Fforasmoche as this court is crediblye enformed that the olde name and companye of organ makers ys nowe consumed and dyssolved, wherefore now at the special request of John Howe ye yonger, organ maker, he is transposed to the mistery and company of skinners.'

That a Guild of organ makers had existed in the City of London in early times is certain, and is shown by various references. Thus, the records of the Worshipful Company of Brewers contain an entry of 1422 concerning a guild of Orglemakers as being one of the 'three crafts exercised from old and still continuing in this ninth year of King Henry V.'

As a musical instrument, the organ has a history of more than 2,000 years, and a 1,000 years of history in England. In the fourteenth century it was considered to be the superior of all other musical instruments. By the sixteenth century organs of considerable quality were being built in England, though it was not before 1660 that organ building became a fully progressive and continuing development.

In the middle ages the British organs were small – markedly smaller than their continental counterparts. In fact, they were small enough to be easily portable, and frequently there was more than one such organ in a large church. At the Church of St

Dunstan in the West one organ was in the 'Quyer' and the other 'in the Rode loffe'.

It is interesting to note that in the earlier days an organ was always referred to as 'a pair of organs' in much the same way as one refers to a pair of shears or scissors.

A rare sixteenth century organ specification which survives concerns an organ made by Antony Duddyngton for the Church of All Hallows, Barking, in 1519.

'The endenture made the yere of our Lorde God MVXIX an the moneth of July xxv day witness that Antony Duddyngton, Citizen of London, Organ Maker, hath made a full barhayn . . . to make an instrument, that ys to say, a payer of organs for the foresed churche of dowble c-fa-ut, that is to say xxvii playne keys and the pryncipale to conteyn the length of v foote so following wt Bassys called Diapason to the same conteyning length of x foot or more: and to be dowble pryncipalls throweout the said instrument, so that the pypes wt inforth shall be fyne metall and stuff as the utter parts that is to say of pure Tyn, wt as fewe stops as may be convenient.'

About the year 1563, when the Puritan movement took a hold on England, many churches did away with their organs. Some were sold to lay purchasers, rich private clients, or innkeepers, others to be broken up. Certainly more than a hundred organs were scrapped and their pipes sold to make pewter plates.

On his visitation to St Paul's Cathedral in 1598 Bishop Bancroft made the following complaint:

'The Orgayns are so misused in the Blowing and other ways wt jogging the bellowes that the bellowes be broken and the winde is not sufficiente to give sownde to the instrument.

'The Organ lofte is greatly abused by ye bell ringers letting up of many people for monye to ye decaye of ye instrument, ye pipes beinge many of them under feete, and ye hazardinge of ye people underneath.'

No doubt there was much of this sort of thing going on in the churches. Bell ringers and organ players were not highly paid, and the opportunity of making a little on the side was not to be ignored.

Henry Purcell, organist at Westminster Abbey, suffered the displeasure of the Chapter for much the same thing, though one may be sure that no damage was thereby caused. Anyway, in 1689 Purcell took money for the admission of spectators to the great organ loft. This came to the ears of the Chapter, who demanded that he hand the money over to them. Furthermore, in their severity, they gave him only two days in which to pay the money, in default of which his position in the Abbey to be declared nul and void. 'And it is further ordered that his stipend of sallary due at our Lady Day last past be detained in the hands of the Treasurer until further notice.'

If the Puritan influence caused the removal of so many organs from the churches, it was the Reformation which preceded it that shattered the wealth of the medieval church in England. It is interesting to consider for a minute the great number of people who were employed by St Paul's in the middle ages. Walter Besant in his *London* presents this remarkable list:

'In the year 1450 the Society, a Cathedral body, included the following: the Bishop, the Dean, the four Archdeacons, the Treasurer, the Precentor, the Chancellor, thirty greater Canons, twelve lesser Canons, about fifty Chaplains or chantry priests, and thirty Vicars. Of inferior rank to these were the Sacrist and three Vergers, the Succentor, the Master of the Singing-school, the Master of the Grammar-school, the Almoner and his four Vergers, the Servitors, the Surveyor, the twelve Scribes, the Book Transcriber, the Book-binder, the Chamberlain, the Rent-collector, the Baker, the Brewer, the singing-men and the choir boys, of whom priests were made, the Bedesmen and the poor folk. In addition to these must be added the servants of all these officers – the brewer, who brewed in the year 1286, 67,814 gallons, must have employed a good many; the baker who ovened every year 40,000 loaves, or every day more than a hundred, large and small; the sextons, grave-diggers, gardeners, bell-ringers, makers and menders of the ecclesiastical robes, cleaners and sweepers, carpenters, masons, painters, carvers and gilders – one can very well understand that the Church of St Paul's alone found a livelihood for thousands.'

As the result of an Order in 1547 all the roods in the parish churches with their attendant images had to be removed. The Order of 1561 brought down the lofts and organs. A huge number of organs were taken away and left to decay. The 1644 Ordinance of the two Houses of Parliament completed the Puritan mission 'for the speedy demolishing of all Organs, images and all matters of superstitious monuments in all Cathedrals, and the Collegiate or Parish-Churches and Chapels, throughout the kingdom of England and the Dominion of Wales, the better to accomplish the blessed reformation so happily begun and to remove offences and things illegal in the worship of God.'

One of the most remarkable organs in the history of English organs was built in the City in the reign of Queen Elizabeth. It was designed and built by Thomas Dallam, an organ-builder by trade and a member of the Blacksmiths' Company.

The purpose of the organ was to be an impressive gift from Queen Elizabeth to the Sultan of Turkey at an opportune time when trade was being opened up in that remote and almost fabled country by the Levant Company. The organ was an extravagant gesture, and in this it was entirely successful.

Unquestionably it was a freak organ, grandiose, and designed to surprise. As one of its additions, there was a 24 hour clock which struck the hours and had a chime of 16 bells. The organ stood sixteen feet high, and on top was a carved holly bush full of thrushes and blackbirds, which 'at the ende of the musick did singe and shake theire wynges.'

The organ case was embellished with two carved figures holding silver trumpets, which they raised to their lips to sound a fanfare. This exceptional organ, so it seems, was also able to play tunes by means of some mechanical contrivance after the manner of a musical box. There was also a keyboard for conventional playing by a musician.

There was also a circular platform on which was mounted a carved figure of Queen Elizabeth, richly set with diamonds and rubies and emeralds. Eight figures deferentially surrounded the figure of the Queen, and above the tableau were the Royal Arms, embossed and gilded and painted. Above that was a carving of a human head surmounted by a cock and supported on either side by a pyramid and a gilded crescent.

An article in the *Illustrated London News* of October 28, 1860 under the title of 'Curious Musical Instrument of the Sixteenth Century', describes the various movements of which the instrument was capable.

'... The first motion, being a clock, shall drive, make to go and move the true course of the sun and of the moon, and shall show the age of the moon truly every day, with her increasing and decreasing; and it shall also show the reigning planets every day very truly.

'The second motion shall move an armed man in another of the towers, and shall strike the quarter of the hour upon a fine, loud and sounding bell. The third motion shall strike the twelve hours of the day in their time upon a greater bell, very loud. The fourth motion shall make the cock to crow very loud every hour, and as often as the director of the said instrument shall appoint; and the same cock shall be made strong, of metal, and shall be very artificially wrought, and made to flutter with his wings.

'The fifth motion shall be in the lower part of the instrument, and shall be a great barrel with a chime of very tunable bells, and shall be made to set to play a chime at any hour, as the person directing the instrument shall dispose. The sixth motion shall make all the persons (the eight figures above described) to go in the presence and make their obeisance to the Queen's Majesty's image, and her personage to move her hand with her sceptre to every one of them as they pass before her.

'The seventh motion shall make the two trumpeters to lift up the trumpets to their mouths and to sound, as often as the director shall set the time. The eighth motion shall move and open the mouth of the great head, and make the eyes thereof to move and turn every hour at the striking of the clock. The ninth motion shall move or turn an hour-glass which an angel shall hold in his hand, and turn it every hour.'

The mechanical aspect of the organ itself is also described.

'There shall be placed in the lower part of the instrument three several strings, forcible and artificial bellows, with a very strong, sufficient motion of wheels and pinions, very well wrought, and sufficient to drive and move the bellows at all times from time to time, for the space of six hours together, whensoever the wheels and pinions shall be applied to such purpose; and there shall be contained within the said instrument a board called a sound-board, with certain instruments or engines called his barrels and keys, and five whole stops of pipes, viz: one open principal, unison recorder, octave principal and a flute, besides a shaking stop, a drum and a nightingale.'

The Illustrated London News informs the reader that the original contract included the clause that the organ should carry with it a seven-year guarantee. The price of the whole thing was to be £550.

This unique organ, constructed in Dallam's workshop in the City, having been completed and put through its paces to the entire satisfaction of everybody, was dismantled and set up again at the Palace of Whitehall for the Queen's inspection and the edification of those who were invited to see it. After that brief period the organ was again taken to pieces and packed in crates and despatched by sea to Turkey, and with it went Dallam and three assistants to set it up for the Sultan on arrival.

Dallam not only survived his very hazardous voyage to Turkey, where he duly installed Queen Elizabeth's organ for the edification of the Sultan, but he in due course returned to the City, to continue his trade as organ-builder.

He built an organ for the Chapel Royal at Holyroodhouse, Edinburgh on the instructions of James I. The case for the organ was designed by Inigo Jones. It was installed in 1617, having been transported from London.

With the assistance of his son, Robert, Dallam built an organ for Durham Cathedral. Robert Dallam also built an organ for York Minster, as well as for a number of churches in Brittany. The City of London organ business of the Dallams was a thriving concern. It is therefore curious to find so successful a citizen of London getting into trouble with his Livery Company. With Thomas Dallam, however, it was a case of professional calls interfering with his civic duties. Thus, he got into trouble with his own Company, the Blacksmiths'.

In the Minute Book of the Court of Assistants of the Blacksmiths' Company is an entry, dated September 29, 1625 to the effect that Thomas Dallon was appointed a steward for the Lord Mayor's feast.

Then comes the entry: 'It was this day ordered that Mr Dallam shall paye his fyne of Tenn pounds for refusing to take upon him to be one of the stewards for the Lord mayors feast next, that if he doe not holde the stewardshepp att the Lord mayors feast come twelve month, that then he shall loose his plaice and if he pays his fyne before, then he shall keep his plaice.'

However, at the following Michaelmas Court Dallam sought to be excused from taking office. The event is duly recorded thus:

'This daye Mr Dallam appeared who was desired to take upon him the stewardshipp at the maiors feast next, who desierde in regard of his buisinis to be spared from holding of it and rather paye his fine, who now laied downe & paied five pounds in part paiement of his fyne of tenn pounds and did agree & promise to paye thother vli as followeth viz, twenty shillings thereof this daye twelvemoneth forty shillings this day two yeres & thother ls residue thereof on this daye three yeares:- which was accepted and soe he is to holde his plaice.'

Not one of Thomas Dallam's organs has survived.

Dr Burney in his *History of Music* says that after the Restoration in 1660 the demand for organs became so great that, because there were so few organ-makers left in the country consequent on the Puritan and Commonwealth policy, great financial inducements were offered to continental organ-builders to come to England.

Bernard Smith (sometimes called Father Schmidt or Father Smith) was an instance of an English organ-builder who had emigrated to Germany during the lean years of the Commonwealth.

Returned to England, Smith produced approximately seventy organs of which two of the most important were those that he built for Wren's St Paul's Cathedral, and the Temple Church.

Undoubtedly, his greatest work was the organ he installed in the Cathedral, and it was there that he became involved in a battle of wills between the Dean of St Paul's and Sir Christopher Wren. Wren wanted the organ to be built into one of the north choir bays; the Dean insisted that Smith's organ should stand on the screen. The Dean overruled Wren's objections.

Smith's organ provided a compass of CCC but Wren dug his heels in and refused to permit the lowest five pipes of the diapasons to be installed; neither would he permit a bassoon or a clarion to be put in. He said bluntly that he was not going to have the beauty of his cathedral spoilt by a damned box of whistles!

Smith, it is said, kept the rejected organ pipes, intending to install them after Wren's death, but as Wren outlived him the completion of the organ never took place.

The organ case was actually designed by Sir Christopher Wren and carved by Grinling Gibbons. Though in these days it is quite usual for an architect to design the organ case – the late Sir

Ninian Comper designed several – the St Paul's case by Wren is probably the first to be so designed.

The records show that Wren had to strengthen the vaulting of the crypt to take the extra weight of the organ, his own plans for the Cathedral not having allowed for the organ to be placed there.

There the organ remained until well into the nineteenth century, when the situation of the organ over the screen became undesirable. Mr Penrose, architect to the Cathedral in studying the Cathedral archives discovered an original drawing by Sir Christopher Wren showing the organ in one of the north choir bays.

In 1872 Wren's organ case was adapted to its present position in one of the north bays, and furnished with the present Henry Willis organ. It is fully recognised today that Wren's proposed siting of the organ was far better than the then Dean's.

Bernard Smith's second London organ of importance was the famous organ he constructed for the Temple Church, which gained considerable notoriety in consequence of the remarkable 'battle of the organs' in 1684.

The story is as follows.

When Bernard Smith proceeded to install his organ in the Temple Church he was fully under the impression that he had been given the contract to install it. It was precisely then that a younger rival in the field of organ building somehow persuaded the Benchers of the Inner and Middle Temple to give him authority to install his own organ in another part of the church. The plan he put up to the Benchers was that after both organs had been tested for a suitable length of time they should decide which organ they thought the better. The name of this enterprising, but not over-scrupulous, rival to Smith was Renatus Harris, who was 23 years Smith's junior.

The rivalry between the two organ-builders went to considerable length during 'the battle of the organs'. Renatus Harris challenged Smith to introduce further reed stops in his organ,

Harris himself being particularly skilled in this feature of organs. This Smith successfully did, no doubt to the chagrin of the younger man, who, on the night before the trial of perfection between the two instruments, caused the bellows of Bernard Smith's organ to be cut, so that it would not work.

That was a curious performance on Harris's part, and one hardly likely to affect the Benchers' judgment of the quality of Smith's organ, which suggests that it was done in a fit of temper.

Anyway, it was not until four years later, in 1688, that after exhaustive tests, the Benchers settled on Smith's organ. But it was a close contest. Voting on the part of the Benchers was equally in favour of both organs, and it required the casting vote of none other than the notorious Judge Jeffreys.

Much of Smith's organ survived in the Temple Church until the dark year of 1940, when it was completely destroyed in the London blitz.

Bernard Smith was a friend of two famous organists, Purcell and Blow. He was also a Fellow of the Royal Society, which in his time included John Evelyn, Isaac Walton, Christopher Wren and John Locke.

Though Renatus Harris lost the Battle of the Organs, he had many successes. He built organs for six cathedrals, and used all his logic and persuasion to build an organ for St Paul's. The idea grew from the organ he had built in Salisbury Cathedral in 1710 'which was begun some years since for a church in London, as a Master-piece of Great Value to have been paid for by Subscription and was made capable of emitting Sounds to express Passion by Swelling and Note as if inspired by Human Breath. But the Place where it is now fix'd not being proper for that Performance, which requires the Situation to be against a Wall, for the Sound to strike but one way, it loses that Advantage; & yet being prepar'd for that Intent, there may be more Varities express'd thereon than by all the Organs in England, were thir several Excellencies united. You are desir'd to observe that the propos'd

Organ for St Paul's is intended to be plac'd at a great Distance from the Choir & not to interfere with the present Organ in the Performance of the Service, being chiefly consider'd in its Situation for the benefit of Swelling the Notes . . .

'The use of it will be for the Reception of the Queen on all public Occasions or Thanksgiving for the good Effects of Peace or War, upon all State Occasions, St Cecilia's Day, the Entertainment of Foreigners of Quality & Artists & on all Times of greatest Concourse . . . '

The organ was to consist of six sets of keys for the hands, besides pedals for the feet. In Harris's own words: 'The first Set to be wholly appropriated for a grand Chorus, intended to be most first & strong that ever has yet been made. The second and third Sets to answer all Sorts & Varieties of Stops & to represent all Musical Instruments. The fourth to express the Echoes. The fifth to be a Choir or Small Organ, yet to contain more pipes & a greater Number of Stops than the biggest Organ in England had at present. The sixth to be adapted for the emitting of Sounds to express Passion by swelling any Note as if inspir'd by Human Breath; which is the greatest improvement an organ is capable of except it had Articulation. On this set of keys the notes will be loud or soft, by swelling on a loud Note or Shake, as the organist's pleasure. Sounds will come surprisingly & harmoniously, as from the Clouds, or distant Parts, pass, & return again, as quick or slow as Fancy can suggest; & be in tune in all Degrees of Loudness & Softness.

'By means of Pedals, the Organist may carry on three Fuges at once, and be able to do as much as if he had four hands, for the Feet would act upon the Pedal-Keys, when the hands were employ'd above, & the Sound would be proportionately strong; which is the grand Chorus in so vast a Church ought to be as strong and bold as possible; and therefore Pedals are us'd in all the Great Organs beyond the seas.'

Renatus Harris's great scheme for an organ at the west end of the Cathedral, though it had the support of Sir Christopher Wren, was never achieved, which, on the face of it, would appear to have been a great musical loss to the City. He certainly did not lack a persuasive tongue in putting forward his great scheme.

A strange man was Harris. His undoubted greatness in organ-building was curiously offset by a streak of pettiness in his nature, as, for example, the damaging of Smith's bellows in the Temple Church. Because of money remaining owing to him, he succeeded in rendering the organ temporarily useless at Christ's Hospital, and at St Clement's church he, for motives of his own, tampered with the organ. John Christopher Smith, Handel's amanuensis and assistant, had the unexpected duty of examining the organ and removing 'the cheat Mr Harris putt into the Organ in order to putt the Organ out of order.'

Harris built the organ for St Bride's Church, Fleet Street, in 1696. It, like Smith's Temple Church organ, perished in the blitz on London. Harris died in 1724.

There appeared in *The Spectator* of February 8, 1712, the following notice:

'Whereas as Messrs Abraham Jordan have, with their own hands, joynery excepted, made & erected a very large organ in St Magnus Church at the foot of London Bridge, consisting of four sets of keys, one of which is adapted to the art of emitting sounds by swelling the notes, which never was in any organ before; this instrument will be publicly opened on Sunday next, the performance by Mr John Robinson. The above said Abraham Jordan gives notice to all masters and performers that he will attend every day next week at the said Church to accommodate all those gentlemen who have a curiosity to hear it.'

It was the 'swell' attachment to which they particularly refer in the above notice, that made the Jordans, father and son, notable organ-builders in England. Though they claimed that the 'swell' was never in any organ before, this was not quite true. The Jordans did not, in fact, invent the device demonstrated in St

Magnus the Martyr, but introduced into England a method already in use in Spain and Portugal.

Mendelssohn's visits to England with his advanced technique caught London and England on the hop! By playing his own works and those of Bach, he emphasised the absolute need for pedals to organs to play the most advanced music. In his youth the favourite pupil of Mozart, Thomas Attwood, Organist at St Paul's, immediately recognised Mendelssohn's merits. He befriended him and entertained at his house at Norwood. He invited Mendelssohn to play the St Paul's organ, which the young musician frequently did.

On one memorable Sunday afternoon in 1829, Mendelssohn played on the Cathedral organ long after the service. The congregation stayed on also, enraptured at Mendelssohn's playing. The vergers, unable to close the Cathedral, at last made the blower let the air out of the organ in the middle of a Bach fugue. The performance ended in an abrupt wail!

Mendelssohn educated the English public in the matter of organ music appreciation. Two other City organs were patronised by this talented man, namely St Peter's, Cornhill, and Christ Church, Newgate Street, both of which had been entirely rebuilt and were well equipped with foot-pedals.

Reproduction of the title page from the first edition of Handel's opera *Rinaldo*. The opera was first produced on 24th February, 1711 at the Queen's Theatre, London

The Haunch of Venison
The date on the music relates to the Lord Mayor of London's inaugural banquet held on November 9th, 1778, the new Lord Mayor being Samuel Plumbe Esq.

CHAPTER 6

EARLY CONCERTS IN THE CITY

The Golden Age of English music lies between the years 1570 and 1645. The splendour of that time can be attributed to a number of causes, but essentially to the country's increasing prosperity, and the virile genius to which England had attained. Then was the Golden Age of learning and literature, of music and poetry and song, and of fearless adventurers – the age of Edmund Spenser and William Byrd, of Francis Bacon, Philip Sidney and Francis Drake, of Purcell and Milton, of Ben Johnson and Shakespeare.

Therefore, it is not surprising that during the latter half of the sixteenth century there came about what in fact were the first public concerts, something hitherto unknown. It was not surprising, too, that this stride forward, this refined innovation of music enjoyment, took place in the City of London, and that the event preceded by a clear hundred years the commonly accepted date of the first concerts.

Eric Blom in his preface to his *Music in England*, makes the observation that 'music in this country has always been largely centralised in the capital.' It has also been said with equal assurance that a history of music in England is a history of music in London. The emergence of public concerts is an example of this.

During the middle ages, music had, in a sense, always been secondary to the main purpose – a means to an end, so to speak, rather than an end in itself. Thus, 'joyful singings' were there to

add lustre to public ceremonial; 'heavenly choirs' were strategic-
ally placed at points on the route to greet the monarch most
advantageously on a royal entry into the City; the noise of
instruments of waits, minstrels, and the King's Musick added
drama and circumstance and pomp to great occasions. Music
during these royal and civic events was a means, too, towards
maintaining a proper appreciation of authority and respectful
obedience on the part of the common people. Nothing was more
calculated to distinguish the great in the land from the common
people than a noise of music to herald their approach and mark
with splendour their passing by.

It was after the close of the middle ages that English music
began to alter its form, and this was brought about by the spread
of humanistic teachings, the Protestant Reformation, and the
actual emergence of a clearly recognisable musical public. Music
was now to be performed for its own sake.

The high degree of musical skill attained by the Waits of the
City undoubtedly inspired the idea of, and made possible, this
new innovation of public concerts.

In the year 1570 the new Royal Exchange building in the City
was completed. This was an occasion of the greatest civic pride,
and the year following the Court of Aldermen gave orders to
the Waits to provide a series of consorts. They were to be public
consorts, played from the building itself.

This was a logical development of the accepted function of the
City Waits, which was to glorify the City and entertain the
citizens, as they had done heretofore by playing their music
during their night watches, at processions, or in consort outside
the houses of the Lord Mayor and the Sheriffs. But this series of
consorts (or concerts, to use the later spelling) was something far
beyond the traditional simple airs to be played on shawms 'with
very cold fingers' during the night hours. The Waits had shown
themselves to be masters of a variety of musical instruments, as
well as in singing. Singing had been a more recent expression of

their talent. They could play in consort with mixed instruments and voices, with sets of shawms, with recorders and sackbuts, with violins and viols, and with lutes.

The order of 1571 by the Aldermen marks the beginning of regular public concerts for the benefit of the citizens of London. That music should be played to the citizens from the turret of the Royal Exchange not only marked an auspicious architectural and political achievement, but also gave a *raison d'etre* for the concerts themselves. The order was 'To play upon their instruments upon the turret of the Royal Exchange every Sunday and holidays towards evening every year from Lady Day (March 25) to Michaelmas.'

On the following year the Aldermen issued instructions for the Waits to hold their concerts every Sunday and holidays from Lady Day to Pentecost, 'as before this time they have been used', from the hours of seven to eight in the evening. With lengthening days and warmer evenings the Waits were directed to play from eight to nine.

Those early public concerts at the Royal Exchange, expressly for the pleasure of the citizens, became a striking feature of City life. There was about it the magic touch of Merrie England, and it lasted for seventy years. But at the end of that time an astringent step was taken in the year 1642, in the reign of Charles I. Brought about by the strong sabbatarian feeling which was prevailing at the time, the Aldermen ordered the Waits 'to cease to play at the Royal Exchange on Sundays as heretofore hath been accustomed. They were, however, to continue the custom on 'every holy day hereafter' as usual, which was something.

Five years after the introduction of the Royal Exchange concerts, in December, 1576, Richard Farrant, who was in charge of the Children of the Chapel Royal, started the first Blackfriars Theatre. It had been intended as a place for rehearsal, but it soon developed into a theatre at which the children put on their own shows before the main show of the evening. The children's performances were very popular with the Court, who made frequent visits to the Blackfriars Theatre. There was a tradition of dramatic production undertaken by the choristers of the several religious establishments in London, including St Paul's.

It was about this time that James Burbage and his associates opened the Theatre at Shoreditch. This was followed by the building of the Curtain Theatre near by. Afterwards came the Bankside playhouses which became famous as the focus point of the leading theatrical companies. The Bankside theatres, too, became places of orchestral music, the musicians who formed the orchestras playing for an hour before the play started, during the *entr'act,* and for half an hour after the show. Sometimes trumpet-blasts heralded the production.

Some of the most famous private musical parties of Elizabethan England in the 1580s gathered at the house of Nicholas Yonge. Yonge, who was a lay clerk of St Paul's Cathedral, compiled the first printed collection of Italian madrigals with English words – the famous *Musica Transalpina.* In his dedication to this work, Yonge refers to the concerts held in his house.

'Since I first began to keep house in this city, it hath been no small comfort unto me, that a great number of gentlemen and merchants of good account (as well of this realm as of foreign nations) have taken in good part such entertainment of pleasure as my poor ability was able to afford them, both by the exercise of music daily used in my house, and by furnishing them with books of that kind yearly sent me out of Italy and other places, which being for the most part Italian songs, are for sweetness of air, very well liked of all.'

It shows clearly that Italian madrigals and the English imitations were popular with the amateur performers at Yonge's musical gatherings. This vogue for Italian part-songs was quickly followed by other composers and translators. The singing of madrigals became a distinctive feature of Elizabethan England.

Yonge's initiative in the madrigal field obtained so wide a

popular response as to encourage him to produce a further *Musica Transalpina, The second booke of Madrigalles, to 5 and 6 voices*. It was published nine years after the first book.

The formation of similar madrigal groups is shown in other dedications. Thus, in Thomas Morley's *Canzonets, or little short songs to foure voyces, collected out of the best and Approved Italian authors*, to 'Master Henrie Tapster, citizen and grocer of the city of London,' Morley thanks Tapster for past courtesies and asks him to accept the songs for 'the honest recreation' of himself and others.

It is clearly apparent that the London of the later years of the sixteenth century had extensive opportunities to enjoy music. St Paul's Cathedral, the Waits of London and the King's Musick, not to mention music in the theatres, all provided their programmes for the musically educated ears of gentlemen. Thus, of the Blackfriars Theatre, a foreign visitor wrote in 1602:

'For a whole hour preceding the play one listens to a delightful musical entertainment on organs, lutes, pandoras, mandoras, viols and pipes, as on the present occasion, indeed when a boy *cum voce tremula* sang so charmingly to the accompanyment of a bass-viol that unless possibly the nuns at Milan may have excelled him, we have not heard his equal on our journey.'

As the Reformation took its course it was to have a profound effect on the music of the country generally. In 1644 the Ordinance for Further Demolishing of Monuments to Idolatory and Superstition decreed that 'all Organs and the Frames or Cases wherein they stand shall be taken away and utterly defaced, and none hereafter set up in their places.'

This, of course, was the work of the Puritans, whose condemnation of instrumental music in places of worship was notorious. In his *History of Music* the celebrated Dr Burney, himself a churchman and a royalist through and through, condemns the Puritans utterly, and not entirely fairly. 'During the Commonwealth the art of music, and indeed all arts but those of killing, canting and hypocrasy, were discouraged . . . Every species of choral music was suppressed.'

That was indeed a statement of prejudice, for it is shown from other sources that the Puritans were in fact music lovers. They practised music in the home, and listened to it with keen enjoyment at the tavern or music club.

As an example of this, Oliver Cromwell himself bought one of the discarded church organs and had it installed at Hinching-brooke. He engaged a music-master to teach his children. Cromwell on one occasion invited the Members of Parliament to 'some rare music' at Whitehall.

Innkeepers and tavern keepers bought up many of the discarded church organs and had them reassembled in their own premises for the entertainment of their guests. Such inns became known as 'music-houses', and the innholders engaged professional musicians to perform for their customers. These music-houses became, in effect, a form of concert hall, with excellent music performed, though in many cases they might be more accurately described as the forerunners of the music hall.

The provision of music at the inn became an accepted custom, and continued throughout the Commonwealth. Moreover, the City Waits were by no means disbanded, though there was a sharp lull during the period of the Civil War. They augmented their income by obtaining additional employment in the city music houses. Sir John Hawkins, peevishly disparaging of the whole set-up of the seventeenth century music houses, and particularly contemptuous of the London Waits, has this to say in his *History of Music*, published in the more elegant days of 1776:

'Fiddlers and others, hired by the master of the house; such as in the night season were wont to parade the city and suburbs under the title of Waits . . . Half a dozen of fiddlers would scrape *Sellinger's Round*, or *John, Come Kiss Me*, or *Old Simon the King* with diversions, till themselves and their audience were tired, after which as many players on the hautboy would in the most harsh and discordant tones grate forth *Greensleeves, Yellow Stockings, Gillian of Croydon*, or some common dance tune, and their people thought it fine music.'

Hawkins is obviously as prejudiced against the waits and music houses as is Burney against the Puritans, for the undeniable truth is that the London Waits of that time were certainly not of such crude talent. They were no bucolic fiddlers, but musicians well able to entertain the cultivated ear of a sophisticated London audience.

The organs may have been banished from the churches, but that secular music suffered no serious set-back during the Commonwealth is shown from contemporary accounts.

John Evelyn wrote in his diary for May 5, 1659:

'I went to visit my brother in London; and next day to see a new opera after the Italian way, in recitative music and scenes, much inferior to the Italian composure and magnificence; but it was prodigious that in a time of such public consternation such vanity should be kept up or permitted.'

This visit, made by Evelyn during the last year of the Commonwealth, was to see a revival of the *Siege of Rhodes* by Sir William Davenant, which opera Evelyn had seen in the most auspicious circumstances in Venice.

Davenant had set himself to establish an English form of opera on the Italian pattern at Rutland House, Charterhouse Square, in 1656. His first production bore the wordy title, *The First Dayes Entertainment at Rutland House by Declamation and Musick: after the Manner of the Ancients*. It was described as an opera; the music is entirely lost. This production was followed by *The Siege of Rhodes*, with stage settings by John Webb, pupil of Inigo Jones.

In *The Siege of Rhodes* John Webb followed the principles employed by Inigo Jones. Depth and perspective was achieved on the stage by a representation of rocks in the foreground, while mid-stage stood a pair of pillars. Supported between the pillars was a painted backcloth, which was held in position in grooves or channels. There were a series of these backcloths bearing picture representation of the various scenes. These could be raised or lowered, and were changed in full view of the audience.

The Restoration in 1660 had an instant effect. The theatres, which had been closed, were opened again with tremendous enthusiasm, and the Restoration comedy came into its own. The same stimulus opened up many musical clubs, which were to flourish right through the eighteenth century, while concerts in taverns and tea gardens became the popular vogue.

To hold private musical evenings were the fashion for those in more affluent circumstances. 'Up betimes,' wrote Pepys in his entry for August 3, 1664, 'and set some joiners at work to new-lay my floor in our Wardrobe, which I intend to make a room for music.' Pepys also took himself off on at least two occasions to musical evenings at the Black Swan, in Bishopsgate, then the Post Office.

Roger North (1653–1734) thus describes the character of concert societies in his *Memories of Musick*. 'The Nation (as I may term it) of Musick was well prepared for a revolution. A great means of bringing that forward was the humour of following public concerts, and it will not be out of the way to deduce them from the beginning. The first of these (in 1664) was given in a lane behind Paul's in the Mitre, where there was a chamber organ that one, Phillips, played upon and some shop-keepers and foremen came weekly to sing in consort, and to hear, and enjoy ale and tobacco; and after some time the audience grew strong, and one, Ben Wallington, got the reputation of a notable bass voice, who set up for a composer, and had some songs in print... this showed an inclination of the citizens to follow music. And the same was confirmed by many little entertainments to masters made voluntarily for the scholars. It being known they were always crowded.'

A song by Pelham Humfrey sung on such a musical occasion

gives a vigorous insight into these pleasantly relaxed occasions:

'How well doth this Harmonious Meeting prove
A Feast of Music is a Feast of Love,
Where Kindness is our Tune, and we in parts
Do but sing forth the Consorts of our hearts.
For Friendship is nothing but consort of votes,
And Music is made by a friendship of notes.

Chorus:

Come then to the God of our Art let us quaff,
For he once a year is reported to laugh.'

During the days of the Puritans a certain Edmund Chilmead, a scholar and an ardent Royalist, was unceremoniously relieved of the chaplaincy he held in Oxford. He came to London and succeeded in earning a living at the Black Horse in Aldersgate Street. The concerts at the Black Horse came under Chilmead's direction. Smoking and drinking at the concerts were an added attraction, and proved a great success.

Public houses were by now accepted as places of English culture. Evelyn records the comments of a French traveller on the sacriligeous manner in which the London innkeepers had 'translated the organs out of the churches and set them up in taverns, chanting their dithyrambics and bestial bacchanalias to the tune of those instruments which were wont to assist them in the celebration of God's praises.'

The Restoration made the widest use of musicians, and French and Italian virtuosos flocked to England and London. Social conditions had so progressed as now to be ripe for the establishment of the public concert, to which the audience paid for the pleasure of listening. The first of this new order of concerts were those arranged in 1673 by a man named John Banister. His name is sometimes spelt Bannister.

Banister was a musician of some talent and a well-known figure, who had composed music for a number of plays. He had been a member of the King's Musick, but according to Pepys he was annoyed by the favourable reception given here to the French violinist Louis Grabu. Roger North, on the other hand, asserted that Banister, then one of Charles II's violinists, had been dismissed from the Royal service for impertinence as well as transferring to his own pocket payments he should have made to his musical subordinates.

Banister had returned to England in 1662 after a musical visit to France, and had been appointed to the King's Musick. Among his duties was to select a very special group of twelve musicians, and he was given money at the rate of £600 per annum to be divided among the elite group of twelve as extra emolument. It was not long, however, before the payments were under question. An enquiry took place, the outcome of which was that Banister was relieved of his office on the grounds that he had retained too much money for himself. The original complaint against Banister was made by the Frenchman Louis Grabu.

The following then appeared:

'Whereas John Banister appointed to make choice of 12 of the 24 violins, to be a select band to wait upon his Majesty, was paid £600 for himself and the 12 violins in augmentation of their wages, His Majesty authorises the payment of £600 to Louis Grabu, Master of His Majesty's Musick, appointed in the place of John Banister . . . '

Banister was not without his own supporters who stoutly argued that the charge brought against him was unfounded, and that the whole thing was a plot. Banister, they insisted, had been dismissed from the post of Master of the King's Musick because he had told the King that the English violinists were superior to the French. This was made in the face of the King's known preference for Continental artists.

Grabu, whose limited musical ability had been spoken about by Pelham Humfrey to Samuel Pepys, remained leader of the band of twelve violinists until 1674.

There appeared in the *London Gazette* of December 30, 1672, the following advertisement:

'These are to give notice that at Mr John Banister's house (now called the music school) over against the George Tavern in White Friars, near the back of the Temple, this Monday, will be music performed by excellent masters, beginning precisely at 4 of the clock in the afternoon, and every afternoon for the future, precisely at the same hour.'

'Banister's room,' says North, 'was rounded with seats and small tables, alehouse fashion. One shilling was the price, and call as you please.' The audience who sat at those tables and called for their drinks and smoked as they listened to the music were mostly local shopkeepers. In the middle of the room was the stand on which sat the instrumentalists. Quaintly, to our way of thinking, the musicians and singers were protected from visual scrutiny by concealing curtains – a style much adopted at that time.

North tells us that 'there was very good music, for Banister found means to procure the best bands in the town and some voices to come and perform there, and there wanted no variety of humour, for Banister did wonders upon a flagelet to a thorough bass, and the several masters had their solos. This continued full one winter, and more I remember not.'

Banister's concerts retained their tavern or music club atmosphere. This was important, as many of his patrons went there to sing as well as listen. Banister was on a sound proposition. Men liked to sing and play together, and the listeners were fully prepared to pay for their entertainment. Furthermore, the professional musicians were readily available: they were 'mercenary teachers, chiefly forreiners'.

John Banister's Whitefriars concerts became the model for ventures of this kind. Foreign musicians seized the opportunities offered by the sudden development of money-making concerts in London and elsewhere.

After a second successful season in Whitefriars, Banister moved outside the City to Covent Garden. Two years after that he established his concerts in Lincoln's Inn Fields. In 1687 he opened up in Essex Street, Strand. He had about him the touch of the showman, invariably advertising his enterprises in the *London Gazette*. Nor did he despise novelty, as example, one of his advertisements informed the musical public of a performance by 'four "trumpets marine", never before heard in England.'

During these pioneer days of the public concert, when Banister and his concerts were proving a popular draw, Thomas Mace in his *Music Monument* (1676) put forward the idea of a public music room, to be erected at public expense. His proposal was that the building should be raised off the ground on stilts to be free of damp and the ill-effects thereof. The musicians were to be accommodated in an area six yards square and, of course, shielded from visual inspection. The audience would be seated in galleries partitioned off from the music room, but able to hear the music by way of apertures bored in the screen! It was never put into effect.

Provided the musical quality was there, concerts were a certain money-spinner, and advertisements appeared regularly in the press. Handbills, too, were much used. During the Banister period and onwards, concert bills were distributed wholesale. They were left in the coffee houses and the taverns, and at the homes of the wealthy and well-to-do, and fly-posted and scattered around in public places.

In fact, these concert bills became such a nuisance that in the year 1700 the Lord Mayor and Aldermen ordered that no bills should be posted in the City on the grounds that they were a public nuisance and encouraged vice and profanity.

North, describing the York Buildings concerts, had the following criticisms to make. 'Here was consorts, fuges, solos, lutes, hautboys, trumpets, kettledrums, and what not, but all disjointed and incoherent, for while ye masters were shuffling out and in of places to take their parts there was a total cessation, and

None knew what would come next; all this was utterly against the true Model of an entertainment, which for want of unity is allway spoiled.'

Bishop Berkeley described the hall in York Buildings as 'the finest chamber I have seen and will contain seats for a select company of 200 persons of the best quality.' Musicians were accommodated in a separate alcove situated at one end of the hall. Dancing schools and the halls of a number of the City Livery Companies were also used for concerts. From 1683 onwards, the Saint Cecilia's Day celebrations took place in the Hall of the Worshipful Company of Stationers.

Charity also played its part in the establishment of concerts. Thus, Charles II granted a Royal Charter of Incorporation to the Charity for the Sons of the Clergy. That was in 1678, and each year the event was marked by a special service in St Paul's Cathedral at which Purcell's *Te Deum* and *Jubilate* were performed. The Feast of the Sons of the Clergy took place in the Merchant Taylors' Hall, and the ticket for that Feast carried with it two Rehearsal Tickets and two Choir Tickets for the actual Festival.

A fund was established for the support of Decayed Musicians, later to be styled the Royal Society for Musicians, and to this charity Handel the composer was a generous contributor.

On almost any pretext of a charitable nature concerts were arranged, as is witnessed by the public press announcements of the day. The *London Evening Post* in 1748 published an advertisement for 'a Grand Entertainment of Musick, Vocal and Instrumental' to assist the victims of 'the late dreadful fire in Exchange Alley'.

The Banister vogue had its repurcussions in other ways, stimulating the vogue for private concert-giving. In his entry of November 20, 1679, John Evelyn makes the following record: 'I dined at the Master of the Mints with my wife, invited to hear Musique which was most exquisitely performed by four of the most renowned Masters, Du Prue a French-man on the Lute: Signor Bartholomeo, an Italian, on the Harpsichord: & Nicolao on the Violin: but above all for its sweetness & novelty the Viol d'Amore of five wyre-strings plaied on with a bow, being but an ordinary Violin, play'd on Lyra way by a German, than which I never heard a sweeter Instrument or more surprising. There was also a Flute douce now in much request for accompanying the Voice: Mr Slingsby, Master of the house (whose Sonn & Daughter played skillfully) being exceedingly delighted with this diversion, had these meetings frequently in his house.'

Signor Bartholomeo was at that time the talk of the town and greatly sought after, both as a harpsichord player and as a teacher. John Evelyn's daughter Mary became one of Bartholomeo's pupils.

Banister's concerts were followed some half dozen years after their formation by the initiative and sheer love of music of one of the most unexpected, remarkable and colourful individuals to be found in the musical history of London. Thomas Britton, the Small Coal man who earned his living by bawling 'Small Coals' in the best London Street Cries tradition as he plodded through the City streets humping his sack of coals (or charcoal) on his back, emerges as one of the most engaging figures in the history of eighteenth century concerts.

Britton's business was in the City streets. His coal store was in Clerkenwell; his heart was in music. He played upon the viola de gamba, and it must be assumed that he played with some skill. Certain it is that he grouped around him lovers of music whose delight was to perform concerted music under his direction. We must, therefore, be for ever indebted to Britton for the cultivation of concert music.

Hawkins in his *General History of Music* finds it quite beyond him to give the socially inferior Thomas Britton his due. In fact, he puts it thus: 'in a very obscure part of the town, viz, at Clerkenwell, in such a place, and under such circumstances as tended to disgrace rather than recommend such an institution. In that it was in the house, or rather hovel, of one Thomas Britton, a man who for his livelihood sold small-coal about the streets . . . '

Hawkins, nevertheless, collected many of the names of those who had attached themselves to the musical soirées of the Small Coal Man and become part of it. There was Banister, there was John Hughes, author of *The Siege of Damascus*, Robe, a Justice of the Peace, Henry Needler of the Excise-office, Wollaston the painter, Henry Symonds, Abiell Wichello, Obadiah Shuttleworth, and Sir Roger l'Estrange.

l'Estrange had the highest regard for the Small Coal Man, whose natural culture and high artistic perception, as well as the generosity of his nature made him a very modest giant in his field of music. It became an honour to be accepted as one of the Britton circle and attend his weekly concerts, which included Handel and the deeply learned John Christopher Pepusch, Organist of the Charterhouse, and who was elected to the Royal Society in 1746. Pepusch arranged the music for Gay's *The Beggar's Opera* and *Polly*. He was invariably there, playing the harpsichord, and it was likely enough that he and Handel first met under Britton's roof. It is said that throughout the spring of 1711 Handel was a regular visitor to the concerts.

Britton was the tenant of a stable, which he divided into two horizontally by building a floor to make an upper room. The ground-floor was his coal store. The upper floor, which was gained by a precipitous outside staircase, formed a long and narrow room which, according to l'Estrange was admirable for musical performance. The unsteady flight of steps was no hindrance to genuine music lovers, which included among its number the lovely Duchess of Queensbury, a celebrated Court beauty, and very regular in her attendance.

Here it was that Thomas Britton, from 1678 to the time of his death in 1714, entertained the musically intellectual society of London to his weekly musical evenings in the narrow, uncomfortable room, in which one could scarcely stand upright.

This he did gratuitously, for a long time refusing to make any charge for his guests. Ultimately he was persuaded to accept a nominal shilling per head.

Britton's musical evenings became the talk of London, and the jealously guarded circle included some of the most distinguished persons in town. All newly-arrived artists in London were ambitious to make their bow at the coal-house concerts of Thomas Britton. Of all the music clubs in London his had pride of place, for it was untouched by commercial enterprise and devoted solely to the art of music. And, so it is said, Handel was happy to play to the mixed company on a little chamber organ with five stops, while the donor of the feast performed upon the viola da gamba.

The respect in which Britton was held was such that he was called 'Sir' by his guests. Wollaston painted two portraits of him, one in which he is shown wearing a kind of dustman's hat, a blouse, and a neckerchief knotted like a rope. On his back is his sack of coal, and in his hand the tin in which to measure it.

Ned Ward describes the Thomas Britton concerts with his customary robust humour and attention to detail in his *Satirical Reflections on Clubs*.

> 'As for the music;
> We thrum the fam'd Corelli's airs,
> Fine solos and sonnetos,
> New riggadoons and maidenfaire,
> Rare jigs and minuettos.
> Sometimes we've a song
> Of an hour or two long,
> Very nicely performed
> By some beau that's so warmed
> With the charms of his Chloe's sweet face
> That he chooses out his love
> Like the amorous dove;
> Which the ladies approve,

And would gladly remove
All the cause of his sorrowful case.'

It was at Britton's that the protégé Matthew Duborg made his debut with, it is suggested by Hawkins, a sonata by Corelli. Corelli ranks very high in the roll of those who laid the foundations of the present art of instrumental composition and performance. He wrote five books of twelve sonatas each, not on what we today call the sonata plan, but, rather, short suites.

In Stoke's *Rapid Plan of Teaching Music* occurs the stanza:

'Of Thomas Britton every boy
And Britain ought to know;
To Thomas Britton, "Small Coal Man",
All Britain thanks doth owe.'

To refer back to Ned Ward once more, he has this to say:

'Upon Thursdays repair
To my palace, and there
Hobble up stair by stair;
But I pray ye take care –
That you break not your shins by a stumble.'

CHAPTER 7

FROM BRITTON TO BURNEY

Britton died in 1714.

Members of every class of society from civil servants to members of the aristocracy, musicians, writers, wits, the famous and the unfamous, made their way each week to his coal store in Clerkenwell just for the sake of his musical evenings, which lasted for thirty years.

With his death ended those remarkable evenings, and at the end of the year his effects were sold, many of them being acquired by Sir Hans Sloane.

Britton's library of music was a valuable acquisition – a hard-working library that had been collected with care and put to practical purposes, and a much thumbed one. It is said that it was from Britton's library that Handel became truly familiar with the traditions of English music and the quality of English music.

There was a gap in the intimate concert world of London when Britton died, but there were other sources of musical inspiration of greater or less importance in the furtherance of concert music.

For instance, in 1689, one of the royal musicians, Robert King, was licensed to hold musical concerts under his own control and with the quaint proviso that 'none shall force their way in, without paying such prices as shall be set down, and no person shall attempt rudely or by force to enter in or abide there during the time of performing the said music.'

Wollaston, the portrait painter, after the break up of the Britton establishment, held Wednesday evening meetings at his house in Warwick Court, off Newgate Street. His guests there were prosperous City men; Wollaston with his close contact with John and Talbot Young, instrument makers, and with Maurice Green and other professionals, was able to provide a first-class series of concerts, both at his home and at the Castle Tavern, Paternoster Row.

Concerning the Castle Tavern concerts, the *Daily Post* of October 17, 1724 gave the following account of the first of them.

'We hear that near one hundred gentlemen and merchants of the City have lately form'd themselves into a musical society, the one part Performers the other Auditors in St Paul's Churchyard. They opened the Consort last week with a very good performance to the entire satisfaction and Pleasure of the members. Mr Young of St Paul's Churchyard, a noted Master of Science, and one of his Majesty's Chapel is President of the Same. As musick must be allow'd to be the most innocent and agreeable Amusement, and a charming Relaxation to the Mind, when fatigued with the Bustle of Business, or after it has been long bent on serious Studies, this bids fair for encouraging the Science, and it seems to be a very ingenious and laudible Undertaking.'

There were in fact three leading subscription concert organisations, of which two were in the City, namely the Castle Concerts, organised by Wollaston, and the Swan Concerts. They took their names from the public houses where they were held. The third was at Hickford's rooms in Brewer Street. The subscription to each was high, which ensured the membership being restricted to the better off classes, and a high standard of professional performance.

The concerts at the Swan Tavern lasted from 1728 to 1740, where such instrumentalists as Obadiah Shuttleworth, Michael Festing and John Clegg performed.

The Castle Concerts began by charging a subscription of two guineas per member, but later were raised to five guineas when, in 1724, oratorio was included. From the Castle Tavern the club concerts were moved to the Haberdashers' Hall and afterwards to the King's Arms in Cornhill. The rules of the Society were first published under the title *The Laws of the Musical Society of the Castle Tavern in Pater-Noster Row. Printed in the year MDCCLI.* They were reprinted in 1759 under the title *The Laws of the Musical Society at Haberdashers' Hall.* They give a very clear insight into the manner in which the concerts were run, and the spirit which prevailed.

Other concerts of a similar nature were held at the Queen's Head in Paternoster Row, and at the Queen's Arms, close by St Paul's. They were much frequented by Handel and Maurice Greene.

At the Angel and Crown in Whitechapel existed another musical association, devoted largely to the music of Purcell, which was organised by a mathematical instrument-maker, a writing master, and a carpenter.

Hawkins describes the concerts held at the house of William Caslon, the type-founder. These concerts took place once a month when the moon was full, which was an obvious boon to those who came to them.

'The performances,' writes Hawkins, 'consisted mostly of Corelli's music intermixed with the Overtures of the old English and Italian operas . . . and the more modern ones of Mr Handel. In the intervals of the performance the guests repasted themselves at a sideboard, which was amply furnished; and when it was over, sitting down to a bottle of wine, and a decanter of excellent ale of Mr Caslon's own brewing, they concluded the evening's entertainment with a song or two of Purcell sung to the harpsichord, or a few catches, and at about twelve retired.'

In 1748 Charles Burney, then 22 years old, came with his wife to live in the City, so as to be near his wife's mother. Burney immediately began to practice as a music teacher. He made a success of it, and in the following year was 'engaged to preside at the harpsichord in a subscription concert then recently established at the King's Arms in Cornhill.' This, of course, was the musical society organised by Wollaston.

This regular engagement was a very useful asset to Burney; he also began to play at other musical sessions held in various City taverns.

On February 26, 1750 there appeared in the *General Advertiser* the following advertisement:

For the Benefit of
Sig. Sanguinette and Sig. Sipruttini
At the King's Arms Tavern (late the Swan) in Cornhill, this Day
February 26th, will be a Concert of Vocal and Instrumental
MUSICK
The Vocal Part by Sig. Gaetano Guadagni from the Opera House;
the first violin and Solo by Mr Jackson; a Solo on the
Violoncello by Sig. Sipruttini,
And an Organ Concerto by Mr Burney
To begin exactly at Half an Hour after Six o'Clock. After
the Concert, by Desire of several Persons of Distinction will be
a BALL
(With proper Musick accompanied with the Tabor and Pipe.)

Another advertisement appeared in the same journal on November 21, 1750:

For the Benefit of Mr Balicourt.
At the Devil Tavern, Temple Bar, on Monday, December 3, will
be performed a Concert of Vocal and Instrumental
MUSICK
The Vocal Part by Miss Stevenson.
The First Violin, with a Solo, by Mr Collett;
A Concerto on the Hautboy by Mr Eiffert;
A Concerto on the Harpsichord by Mr Burney;
A Concerto on the Violoncello by an eminent Master, and
The German Flute by Mr Balicourt.

In Burney's early days in the City he and his wife were living with Dr and Mrs Arne. It was then that Burney got to know Arne's famous sister, the actress Mrs Cibber, and through her met Garrick. Burney and Garrick remained close friends.

After the Castle Concerts had ceased, though the exact date is not known, similar concerts went on with unabated success in other taverns in the City. Henry Angelo (born 1760) has this to say of City concerts in the 1780s.

'About this period there were several musical societies and concerts, held at certain taverns on the east of Temple-bar. I remember one, at the Old Queen's Arms tavern, situated on the north side of Newgate-street, to which on Thursday nights, admission was obtained by tickets at two shillings each. The performers at this time were in part professional and others were amateurs. Here Shore, the renowned trumpet, used to perform, and Fischer occasionally gave them a solo on his oboe – two such players as may not be heard again for a hundred years. Here, as I have been informed, at one period, Corelli's quartets were played in genuine style . . . '

In the *Reminiscences of Henry Angelo* the author makes reference to the Mulberry Tree Club which held its musical evenings at a coffee house in Bow Street. He tells us that the members of the club, and any of the public who bought tickets, dined together at about 3 o'clock on Saturdays. Singers from the theatres formed the bulk of the members, and they provided their own entertainment. Matt Williams, the proprietor of the coffee house, was himself a professional actor and very popular, and it was no doubt his personal popularity that caused so many professionals to rally round him in his enterprise.

What were known as Glee Clubs came into existence in the City in the last twenty years of the eighteenth century, and continued well into the middle of the nineteenth. At the meetings of The Glee Club at the Newcastle Coffee House, which were held on alternate Saturday evenings, the glees to be sung were chosen by seniority, starting with the officials of the club and then the members in order of seniority. The club continued until 1857.

Glee clubs were essentially for male singers. All the members were expected to sing, whether professionals or amateurs, but from the records it would seem that in time non-singing members were added, who occupied themselves with listening to the others, and contentedly refreshing themselves with food and drink.

Among the most famous of the musical ventures started in the City was undoubtedly the Madrigal Society, which still exists. It began in the Twelve Bells, a tavern in Whitefriars, and in the year 1742 limited its membership to sixteen. The members paid a quarterly subscription of three shillings. There was also a fine of sixpence levied on any member who started to eat his supper during practice time. The sixpences so collected were spent in buying ruled music paper on which to make the copies of the madrigals.

The pattern of the evening was standardised into two singing sessions, in each of which four madrigals were to be sung. There was half an hour's interval between the two sessions. According to the club rules 'All musical performances shall cease at half an hour after ten o'clock, unless some of the members shall be cheerfully incited to sing catches, in which case they shall be indulged for half an hour and no longer.'

Burney, occupied as he was with his large music-teaching practice, his concert work, and considerable social proclivities, added to his employment by playing in theatre orchestras, in which he was assisted by Arne. He also gained the post of organist at the church of St Dionis, Backchurch, which stood at the corner of Fenchurch Street and Lime Street.

After the Great Fire of London the church had been rebuilt to the designs of Christopher Wren, and the organ built by Renatus Harris, though whether by Harris senior or junior is a debated point.

There were nine candidates for the post of organist. During

August and September the aspirants for the post took it in turns to play every Sunday morning and afternoon. In October the vestry voted, and out of a total of 55 votes 50 went to Burney.

Dr Percy A. Scholes, author of *The Great Dr Burney*, expressed the view that before being installed in the position of organist of a City church, Burney must have been made a member of some City Company. Dr Scholes based this suggestion on extracts made from *The British Journal*, 1724 in which legal proceedings took place between the City Musicians Company and the organist at St Giles's Cripplegate, turning on the question of whether music is a trade or a science. It represents a test case, the verdict of which could have equally affected Burney.

'*2nd May*, 1724 A remarkable Tryal was to have come on last Tuesday at Guildhall, between City Musicians and the ingenious Mr Green, organist at Cripplegate, a Blind Gentleman, for his exercising the Art of Musick in the City without being free. But the same was put off to the 23rd of May.

'*18th July*. On Tuesday, was try'd in the Lord Mayor's Court at Guildhall, the Cause between the Chamberlain of London, Plaintiff, and Mr Green, a Blind Gentleman, Organist of St Giles's, Cripplegate. Defendant, on account of the latter's practising Music in the City for Gain, without being a Freeman; the Prosecution was grounded on an Act of Common Council made in the Fourth Year of King James I, which lays a Penalty of Five Pounds on any person presuming to exercise any Manual Occupation within the City, not being free thereof.

'It was insisted in his Defence, that Musick was a Liberal Science, and therefore not restrain'd by that Law. But a Distinction being made by the Plaintiff's Counsel, between the scientific Part and the manual Part, a Verdict was given in favour of the Plaintiff.

25th July. On Tuesday last Mr Green, Organist of St Giles's, Cripplegate, was presented to the Lord Mayor and Court of Aldermen; and the next Day admitted a Member of the Company of Leather-sellers and made a Freeman of the City of London: which Freedom he had purchas'd, that he may continue his Business in this City.'

It was proved necessary for Mr Green to be a Freeman of the City to practice as an organist in the City, but it was seemingly immaterial what Company. No doubt the matter was automatically and satisfactorily arranged in Burney's case when he became organist at St Dionis', Backchurch.

Incidentally, St Dionis' was a City church attended by Pepys, and which he naively mentions in his Diary: 'Up (my wife's eye being ill still of the blow I did in a passion give her on Monday last) to church alone.' Of the congregation at St Dionis' Pepys observes, 'very great store of fine women there in this church, more than I know anywhere about us.'

CHAPTER 8

HANDEL IN LONDON

When Handel came to London for the first time, in the year 1710, it was to the capital of a country that had won the battles of Blenheim and Ramillies, that was on top of the world, but whose musical prowess had attained a depth of mediocrity.

English music was indeed at its lowest. Foreign musicians of very average ability swarmed into London, and bad opera was the fare of the theatres. The great days of Henry Purcell had faded in the fifteen years that had elapsed since his untimely death. Had Purcell lived he might well have saved English music from the overwhelming pressure of Italian opera; he might have tempered the powerful influence of Handel, which was so to turn the course of English music into new and exotic channels.

That Purcell died when he did remains a lasting regret to the discriminating in music. He had still so much to give to the purely English form of music. This is not to decry Handel, whose greatness no one would wish to deny, but only to suggest that if events had turned out differently, and perhaps Purcell had lived to his full span, English musical genius would have created opera as well as anybody.

Arne, Boyce and Greene do not possess the depths that lie in Handel's music, but their music is closer to the spirit of England and the English genius. Handel is inevitably more of a cosmopolitan. But he came to England when England was a musical desert.

Not long before he died, Purcell wrote. 'Music is yet in its nonage, a froward child which gives hope of what he may be hereafter in England, when the masters of it shall find more encouragement. It is now leaving Italian, which is its best master, and studying a little of the French air to give it somewhat more of gaiety and fashion.'

On his death in 1695, *The Flying Post* records a Resolution of the Chapter of Westminster Abbey.

'Mr Henry Purcell, one of the most celebrated Masters of the Science of Musick in the kingdom and scarce inferiour to any in Europe, dying on Thursday last; the Dean of Westminster knowing the great worth of the deceased, forthwith summoned a Chapter, and unanimously resolved that he shall be interred in the Abbey, with all the Funeral Solemnity they are capable to perform for him, granting his widow the choice of the ground to reposit his Corps free from any charge, who has appointed it at the foot of the Organs, and this evening he will be interred, the whole Chapter assisting with their vestments; together with all the Lovers of that Noble Science, with the united Choyres of that and the Chappel Royal, when the Dirge composed by the Deceased for her late Majesty of Ever Blessed Memory, will be played by Trumpets and other Musick . . . '

George Frideric Handel was Capellmeister to the Elector of Hanover, after having studied in Italy, where he acquired a high reputation as a performer on the harpsichord and organ. Handel's first visit to England lasted nearly a year. Dr Burney observes that his reception was 'as flattering to himself, as honourable to the nation'. He moved in the highest circles, admired and courted, and in his own turn loved the life of London.

His way of life was simple and unaffected. He delighted to mix with the St Paul's choir at the Queen's Arms Tavern in St Paul's Churchyard where he passed the evening once a week playing on the harpsichord, talking and drinking beer.

It was said of Handel that in two years he became fluent in Italian, yet the greater part of his lifetime, spent in London, he always spoke bad English with a strong German accent. Handel, too, was a considerable humorist and story-teller, but it required a knowledge of four languages to understand them, for he mixed up his German, French, Italian and English regardless!

His opera, *Rinaldo*, was Handel's first work in England, and its production on February 24, 1711, made Handel famous throughout London. The libretto was banal to a degree, but the music was a wonder and delight, spontaneous, charged with youth and vitality. The barren years since the death of Purcell were rolled back. There was nothing like the genius of Handel, the German Capellmeister to the Elector of Hanover, with his Italian musical training and a profound love of England. Handel composed *Rinaldo* in a fortnight.

It seems that only Addison, the essayist, was hostile to *Rinaldo*. But that was because of the failure of his own *Rosamund*, which ran for only three performances. Addison derided the successful foreigner, yet though he attacked *Rinaldo*, the only serious criticism he was able to bring to bear with any validity concerned the novelty feature of the opera, when hundreds of wild birds were let loose at one point in the plot, snuffing out the candles, and a danger to the heads of the audience!

John Jacob Heidegger, a Swiss of German descent who was for many years to manage Handel's opera productions in London, introduced him into London Society. Among others Heidegger introduced Handel to Sir John Stanley, a Commissioner of Customs, at Stanley's house. Mary Granville, at the time only ten years old and Stanley's niece, later to become Mrs Delaney and a close friend of Handel's, recalled that first meeting in later years.

'In the year '10 I first saw Mr Handel who was introduced to my uncle by Mr Heidegger, the . . . most ugly man that was ever formed. We had no better instrument in the house than a little spinet of mine, on which the great musician performed wonders. I was much struck with his playing, but struck as a child, not a judge, for the moment he was gone, I seated myself at my instrument and played the best lessons I had then learnt. My uncle archly asked me if I thought I should ever play as well as Mr Handel. "If I did not think I should," I cried, "I would burn my instrument!" Such was the innocent presumption of childish ignorance.'

Heidegger was on one occasion the victim of an elaborate practical joke. Himself a *bon viveur*, he was taken one day to the Devil's Tavern at Temple Bar, where his companions proceeded to make him helplessly drunk. When he was reduced to a state of total intoxication and quite motionless a cast was taken of his face.

A masquerade was being held at the King's Theatre some days afterwards. Heidegger was there and suddenly found himself confronted by a man who was his double. A mask had been made from the cast and was now being worn by Lord Montague. But Heidegger only laughed; he was completely unperturbed at the sight of his own ugliness. It was even thought that he was rather proud of being considered the ugliest man in London.

After his first year's stay in London Handel somewhat reluctantly returned to his duties in Hanover, but after a short spell there sought permission of the Elector once more to visit London. This he was allowed to do in the autumn of 1712, having first promised that he would not long absent himself from his duties in Hanover.

London, however, proved too strong for Handel. The musical world hailed his return as logical and a national acquisition. He was called upon to compose a *Grand Jubilate* and *Te Deum* to mark the Peace of Utrecht.

The Thanksgiving Service, at which the two compositions were to be the highlight, was to be held at St Paul's Cathedral. *The Post Boy* of July 2, 1713, announced that 'Her Majesty, accompanied by the Houses of Lords and Commons, goes the 7th to St Paul's, being the day appointed for the thanksgiving.'

But on this occasion at least Queen Anne, it seems, was no respecter of persons. Instead, she exercised the woman's prerogative to change her mind. *The Post Boy* of July 4 published the following: 'Her Majesty does not go to St Paul's, July 7th, as she designed, but comes from Windsor to St James's to return thanks to God for the blessings of peace.'

Nevertheless, Queen Anne, as a reward for his *Grand Jubilate* and *Te Deum*, settled on Handel a life pension of £200 per annum.

It seems pretty certain that Handel was a frequent and honoured member of the musical coterie that met weekly in the stable premises of Thomas Britton, the Small Coal Man, where he played on the little chamber organ with five stops. That was the life he loved – good company, good music, good beer!

He became an eager citizen of London, attending the concerts at the Swan and the Crown, and with the choristers of St Paul's at the Queen's Arms. He was a constant visitor, too, at St Paul's, shouldering his way through the itinerant vendors crowding the West Door and shouting their wares, to listen to the organ and Purcell's music.

It was there, too, that he first made friends with Richard Mears, who was to become his music publisher. Mears had started his publishing business some ten years before, and his shop, 'The Golden Viol', was at the top of Ludgate Hill. He was a well-known and popular figure in the Queen's Arms tavern and where else the musical coteries met for concert music.

With all this, Handel forgot, or preferred to ignore, his promise, and did not return to Hanover. Then Queen Anne died and the Elector of Hanover came to London as George I.

He succeeded to the Throne of England August 1, 1714. He arrived in London from Hanover September 18, and was crowned at Westminster on October 20.

Popular legend has it that George I's annoyance with Handel was such that he ignored his presence completely. It has been also said that the King 'was all the more irritated against his truant Capellmeister for having written the *Te Deum* on the Peace of

Utrecht, which was not favourably regarded by the Protestant princes of Germany.'

Popular legend also affirms that 'a Hanoverian baron named Kilmanseck, a great admirer of Handel and a close friend of George I, undertook to bring the two together again. Being informed that the King intended to picnic upon the river Thames, he requested the artist to compose a piece for the occasion. Handel wrote twenty-five little pieces of concerted music known under the name of *Water Music*, and caused them to be executed in a barge which followed the royal boat.

'The orchestra was somewhat numerous; for it consisted of four violins, one viol, one violoncello, one counter-bass, two hautboys, two French horns, two flageolets, one flute, and one trumpet. King George had no difficulty in recognising the author of the symphonies, and he felt his resentment against Handel begin to soften.

'Shortly afterwards, Geminiani, the violinist, a celebrated pupil of Corelli's school, was about to play in the King's private cabinet some snatches which he had composed, but fearing that they would lose much of their effect if they were accompanied in an inferior manner he expressed a desire to be assisted by Handel. Kilmanseck carried the request to the King, supporting it strongly with his own recommendation; and eventually George I consented, and, to seal the peace, added a pension of £200 to that already held.'

Here, then, is the legend as told by Handel's biographer, Victor Schoelcher, of the musician being reconciled to his master by means of a plot to produce the *Water Music* on a warm August evening in the year 1715 on the idyllic waters of the Thames. Hawkins also subscribes to the same date, on the authority of a friend of Handel's.

There is a contemporary account by Malcolm of the Thames picnic.

'August 22, 1715. The King, the Prince and Princess of Wales, and a large party of nobility, went in barges with music from White Hall to Limehouse. And when they returned in the evening, the captains of shipping suspended lanterns in their rigging, and the houses on both sides of the river were illuminated, and an incredible number of boats filled with spectators attended the Royal Party, and cannons were continually fired during the day and evening.'

Another splendid acquatic procession of a similar nature took place on the Thames in July 1717, and it was for this latter occasion, according to Malcolm's account, that Handel expressly composed his *Water Music*.

Schoelcher claims that in this Malcolm was mistaken. The *Water Music* was possibly repeated in 1717, but it was definitely written for the party of August 1715.

A much later biographer, Newman Flower, is quite sure that Handel's *Water Music* was played for the first time in 1717. Newman Flower bases his claim on a document discovered in the Berlin archives, which was a report made by the Brandenburg envoy to the English Court, Frederic Bonnet, and dated July 19, 1717.

The Report, given by Newman Flower in his *George Frideric Handel* (Cassel 1923. Fourth Edition 1964) and translated into English, is as follows:

'Some weeks ago the King expressed a wish to Baron von Kilmanseck to have a concert on the river, by subscription like the masquerades did this winter which the King attended assiduously on each occasion. The Baron addressed himself therefore to Heidegger, a Swiss by nationality, but the most intelligent agent the nobility could have for their pleasures. Heidegger answered that as much as he was eager to oblige his Majesty, he must reserve the subscription for the big enterprises, to wit, the Masquerades, each of which was worth from £300 to 400 guineas to him.

'Baron Kilmanseck, seeing that H.M. was vexed about these difficulties, resolved to give the concert on the river at his own expense, and so the concert took place the day before yesterday. The King entered his barge about eight o'clock with the Duchess of Bolton, the Countess of Godolphin, Madame du Kilmanseck, Madame Were, and the Earl of Orkney, gentleman of the King's Bedchamber who was on guard.

'By the side of the Royal Barge was that of the musicians to the number of fifty who played all kinds of instruments, *viz*, trumpets, hunting horns, oboes, bassoons, German flutes, French flutes á bec, violins and basses, but without voices. This concert was composed expressly for the occasion by the famous Handel, native of Halle, the first composer of the King's music. It was so strongly approved by H.M. that he commanded it to be repeated, once before and once after supper, although it took an hour for each performance.

'The evening party was all that could be desired for the occasion. There were numberless barges, and especially boats filled with people eager to take part in it. In order to make it more complete Madame du Kilmanseck had made arrangements for a splendid supper at the pleasure house of the late Lord Ranelagh at Chelsea on the river, to where the King repaired an hour after midnight. He left there at three, and at half-past four in the morning H.M. was back at St James's. The concert cost Baron Kilmanseck £150 for the musicians alone, but neither the Prince nor the Princesses took any part in the festivities.'

A contemporary report of the occasion appeared in the *Daily Courant* of July 29, 1717, and agrees with that made by the Brandenburg envoy.

'On Wednesday evening at about eight the King took water at Whitehall in an open barge, wherein were also the Duchess of Bolton, the Duchess of Newcastle, the Countess of Godolphin, Madame du Kilmanseck, and the Earl of Orkney, and went up the river towards Chelsea. Many other barges with persons of quality attended, and so great a number of boats, that the whole river in a manner was covered. A City Company's barge was employed for the music, wherein were fifty instruments of all sorts, who played all the way from Lambeth, while the barges drove with the tide without rowing as far as Chelsea, the finest symphonies, composed expressly for the occasion by Mr Handel, which His Majesty liked so well that he caused it to be played over three times in going and returning. At eleven His Majesty went ashore at Chelsea, where a supper was prepared, and then there was another very fine consort of music, which lasted till two, after which His Majesty came again into his barge and returned the same way, the music continuing to play until he landed.'

Well, it would seem that the legend and the facts concerning the *Water Music* will never be entirely separated, but the picture of the sycophantic Kilmanseck in the guise of the altruistic go-between in the unlikely estrangement between the King and Handel is highly suspect.

According to Newman Flower, Kilmanseck was a philanderer who fawned at the King's feet, and his position at Court, though technically that of Master of the Horse, was little better than that of husband to the King's favourite mistress, Madame Kilmanseck. Kilmanseck spent his riches in trying to ingratiate himself with a master who granted few favours in return, and so no doubt had a supreme contempt for him.

The absence of autographed manuscripts of the *Water Music* makes it very hard to decide what was played when.

It seems reasonable to suppose that both the Royal Water Parties, that of 1715 and 1717 were enlivened by *Water Music* by Handel. River parties of such a nature were frequent and highly popular events. The Thames lent itself to such diversions. The river was wide and quiet and smooth, and the air was fresh. It compared well with the streets.

Public wherries, private boats and barges, passed to and fro, gay and colourful. At night the scene would be reminiscent of Venice, the great houses by the waterside with their terraces and steps down to the river lighted by lamps and torches. The Thames was still London's greatest attraction as well as its greatest highway, whether it was for the King or the Lord Mayor or the people.

Regarding Handel himself and the *Water Music*, the King may well have been vexed at his failing to return from London to Hanover, but at the same time he could not fail to recognise the important fact that his Cappelmeister was the doyen and leader of London's musical fashion, and that his genius was undisputed. That alone strengthened the King's own position on a throne the lasting qualities of which, so far as he was concerned, he had the gravest doubts!

The truth is that far from ignoring Handel's presence, within a few weeks of his arriving in London the King came incognito to see *Rinaldo*, which had been revived to add to the Coronation festivities in October. The King also went to see on several occasions during 1715 Handel's new opera, *Amadigi*.

Handel's *Water Music* was not published until 1732 or '33. Today it seems certain that it was *not* composed in its entirety for one occasion, but rather that the music was heard in part in 1715, and that later music on the same theme was played on the 1717 occasion.

Despite his London popularity, Handel nevertheless had his detractors. Alexander Pope, the poet, was a case in point. He moved in the same circle, but was not impressed with Mr Handel, whose indifferent English, flavoured with a strong German accent, irritated him.

Alexander Pope was tone-deaf; he had no more ear for music than had Dr Johnson. Because of this he had an actual distaste for music. He also had a hearty distaste for foreign musicians, and derided opera. His inherent attitude, therefore, towards Handel was one of suspicion tinged with contempt. He was, however, far too shrewd a man unduly to show it, and was wise enough to doubt his own judgment.

Instead, he went to Dr Arbuthnot, his friend and also a friend of Handel's, and asked him point blank concerning Handel's reputation; was the rapture evinced by his audience genuine or merely a frivolous fashion.

Replied Arbuthnot: 'Conceive the highest you can of his abilities, and they are far beyond anything you can conceive.'

Pope accepted Arbuthnot's reply, but confessed that 'Handel's finest performances give me no more pleasure than the airs of a common ballad singer.'

Dr Johnson's attitude towards music was almost identical with that of Pope, and he tended, like others with the same disability, to speak slightingly of both music and those who followed it. It was only in consequence of becoming well acquainted with Dr Burney that he realised his error in indulging in an attitude of mind so unworthy of his liberal judgment.

When Burney said to him on one occasion, 'I even hope, Sir, I shall some time or other make you, also, sensible of the power of my art,' Johnson replied: 'Sir, I shall be very glad to have a new sense put into me!'

But Pope was not liberal-minded at all, and it is quite certain that he at times slighted Handel, while Swift ridiculed him. Handel frequently met them at Dr Arbuthnot's house, where he also met Gay and Congreve.

On February 14, 1726 Handel, the Anglophil, went to the House of Lords to swear an oath of allegiance to this country. Six days later the King put his signature to the Bill that turned his erstwhile Capellmeister into a British subject.

On January 29, 1728, the production of *The Beggar's Opera* took place at the Little Theatre in Lincoln's Inn Fields. By preceding Handel's premiere of *Sirce* by some three weeks it took the wind badly out of Handel's sails. Gay and Pepusch between them had pulled off exactly the kind of entertainment that London needed. It was a break from Italian opera with their often turgid or purile plots. It was gay, it was tuneful, and it was in the English spirit. In a sense the music was a 'Fancy'. Pepusch and Gay had borrowed all the most engaging melodies and written

Gay's words to them. They drew on Purcell, and with utter impudence took Handel's grand march from *Rinaldo* and turned it into the roystering highwayman's song 'Let us take the road'.

There was an old custom for celebrating St Cecilia's day (November 22) with music. In 1683 began the series of festival services held in a City church on that day. There would also be given a public performance at Stationers' Hall of an ode in praise of the Saint and the art of music. In 1739 Handel's *Ode for St Cecilia's Day* was played to crowded houses.

When George II returned after the victory at Dettingen in which the Austro-English army commanded by the King had been rescued from almost certain ruin, Handel began immediately to compose his *Dettingen Te Deum*, and shortly afterwards his *Dettingen Anthem*. When the *Te Deum* was performed at the Chapel Royal on November 27, 1743, every kettledrum and every trumpet that could be found was used for the occasion. The effect was tremendous, martial and stately, and the King was deeply moved.

When the Hymn was performed at the Commemoration of 1748 it was done with 'fourteen trumpets, two pairs of common kettle drums, two pairs of double drums from the Tower, and one pair of double bass drums made expressly for the Commemoration.'

Music for the Royal Fireworks was an occasion which had a gratifying dress-rehearsal in Vauxhall Gardens. The official occasion was in Green Park on Thursday, April 27, 1749, and nearly ended disastrously, consequent on an enormous set catching alight. 'The Machine,' reported the *Gentleman's Magazine* for that month, 'was situated in the Green Park, 500 feet from his Majesty's Library, and represented a magnificent Dorick temple, from which extended two wings, terminated by pavilions, 114 feet in height, to the top of his Majesty's Arms 410 feet long. Invented and designed by the Chevalier Servandoni. Disposition of the fire-works: after a grand overture of warlike instruments, composed by Mr Handel, a signal was given for the commencement of the fire-works, which opened by a royal salute of 101 brass ordnance, viz., 71 six-pounders, 20 twelve-pounders, and 10 twenty-four pounders.'

After that things went wrong. The 'machine' caught fire, and the Royal Library only just escaped being burnt. The occasion was to celebrate the peace of Aix-la-Chapelle, which was concluded October 7, 1748.

CHAPTER 9

THE BEAT OF DRUM

The Handbook of Ceremonials of the City of London, 1906, has this to say about soldiers:

'Whenever it is necessary for troops to pass through the City of London, the Secretary of State for the Home Department writes to the Lord Mayor to inform him thereof, and to request the sanction of the Authorities of the City of London for the troops marching through it.'

The same *Handbook of Ceremonials* has also this to say:

'The Royal London Militia, now the 6th Battalion of the Royal Fusiliers, which was originally raised from the trained bands of London, have the privilege of marching through the City with bayonets fixed and colours flying.

'The Honourable Artillery Company claim and have exercised the same privilege.

'There is one regiment of infantry, the "East Kent", formerly known as the 3rd, or "Buffs", which, in consequence of having been originally formed from the trained bands of London has been allowed the privilege to march through the City of London with bayonets fixed and colours flying.'

The origin of permission to march through the City of London with drums beating is due, except in the case of the Honourable Artillery Company, to the regiments shortly after the Restoration being allowed to *recruit* 'by Beats of Drum'.

We thus see that the City, careful in all matters affecting itself, is careful in its attitude towards the display of armed strength and the accompanying beat of drum in its streets, and only on its own terms.

The citizen soldiers of London date from the time when the Plantagenet King Henry III (1216–1272) ordered the Mayor to raise a body of armed and disciplined men for the defence of the City. The men were duly picked, armed, and warned to muster 'at the tolling of St Paul's bell.'

In the same reign was instituted the Marching Watch, and this was maintained until the reign of Edward VI – a period of approximately 200 years. It was a very sizeable force, comprising 2,000 well-armed men. Their uniform was of white fustian, bearing the arms of the City on back and breast, and the citizen force marched through the streets on the vigils of St John the Baptist and St Peter, to the sound of martial music, and carrying torches.

Henry VIII came to the City to see for himself what was described as 'the pompous march of the City Watch'. The Lord Mayor, so we are told, was attended by a giant and two pages on horseback. This splendid procession marched past the King, illuminated by 940 cressets borne aloft on poles. The cressets were vessels of iron made to hold grease or oil to be burned for light. The Watch consisted of archers – 'honest persons with bows and arrows cleanly harnessed and arrayed in jackets of white with the arms of the City' – pikemen, billmen, and halberdiers, with a body of demi-lances in bright armour.

A document of that time (1538) describes the Honourable Artillery Company by its Charter title of 'Maysters Rulers and comynaltie of the Fraternitye or Guylde of Artyllary of Long-bowes Crossbowes and handegonnes.'

A year later, on May 8, 15,000 picked men, 'clenely hosed and shodde' in white, and each man armed with a sword and dagger, marched to Westminster, where they were reviewed by the King.

The column was headed by pieces of cannon in gun-carts with powder and gun-stones (stone cannon-balls) in carts behind them. Then followed hand-gunners, bowmen, pikesmen and billmen. The musketeers as they passed the King saluted him with volleys, while the great guns were drawn up and 'shotte very terribly in divers places and especially before the King.'

When troops were being sent for service in Ireland, in 1585 Queen Elizabeth wrote to the Lord Mayor: 'Whereas not long since we willed our pleasure unto you for the putting in order of 2,000 armed pikes and 2,000 shot *to be sorted into bands* under Captains. These shall be to authorize you to make the said levy.' It was from this date and letter that the term 'Trained Bands' came into general use.

On all these marches and reviews of the City's own soldiers there was military music, particularly drums and fifes, as at the funeral of Sir Philip Sidney in January, 1587. A contemporary manuscript at the College of Arms describes the 'Cyttizins of London Practised in Armes, about 300, who marched 3 by 3 . . . After them followed the 'Muskiters 4 rancks, drums and fyfs, small shott 20 rancks, pykes 20 rancks, halberds 4 rancks', etc.

In 1638, at Merchant Taylors' Hall, an exercise was performed by 'Certain Gentlemen of the Artillery Garden' before many of the 'Nobility, Aldermen and Gentry'. According to the *History of The Honourable Artillery Company, 1537–1947*, by G. Goold Walker, 'The proceedings opened with a display and combat by eighteen "Targettiers", armed with morions, swords and targets, who "made their encounters and varied their figures all according to the distinct sounds of their musick". Then entered twenty-two members disguised as Saracens . . . "their musick was a turkie Drumme and a hideous noise-making pipe made of a Buffolas horn' . . .

'Next appeared forty members "in the Moderne Armes", namely, "sixteen Musketiers in Buffe-Coats and Beaver Morians, sixteen Pikemen, one Phife and two Drummes", with officers and sergeants. They marched round the hall, "the Drums beating a lofty English march", after which the drums "struck an Alt", . . .

'The whole body then performed a multitude of "postures" of the pike and musket to a "posture tune" played by the fife. These were followed by a series of complicated evolutions . . . performed to "the streyn of the Almain posture tune" . . . '

In 1731 the 'Grenadier music' of the Honourable Artillery Company 'consisted of one curtal, three hautboys and no more'. The curtal was an instrument resembling a small bassoon. In 1762 the music of the Company was made up of 'two trumpets, two French horns, two bassoons and four hautboys or clarinetts'. These instruments, it is recorded in the history of the band of the H.A.C. were played by Germans.

The prized privilege of the Honourable Artillery Company is that of marching under arms with drums playing through the City. But it is a jealously guarded privilege. When, in 1769, a detachment of the Guards, returning to the Tower after suppressing a riot at Spitalfields, did that same thing there was a very sharp response. The Lord Mayor wrote to the Secretary of War with the strong complaint that the Guards had marched through the City with drums beating, fifes playing, and generally making 'a very war-like appearance, which raised in the minds of peaceable citizens the idea of a town garrisoned by regular troops.'

In his reply the Secretary of War promised to deal with the officer of the offending party to prevent any similar offence being given to the City or its Chief Magistrate in the future.

The Tower of London itself is not within the jurisdiction of the City, being a Royal Castle. Thus, though there is always a garrison at the Tower there is not thereby a garrison in the City. It is a fine distinction, but an exact one.

A more light-hearted incident occurred in 1745 when a detachment of troops marched along Cheapside to the beat of drum. They were peremptorily stopped by an Alderman, who addressed the officer in command, and insisted that they ceased playing.

'Sir,' said the officer, 'we are Marines, not soldiers.'

'I beg your pardon,' replied the Alderman. 'I did not know. Pray continue your march as you please.'

It should be remembered that in those days the army was far from popular with the general public, and anything that might savour of a recruiting campaign was severely frowned on by the City of London.

Nevertheless, there were special occasions when the drums of regiments other than the H.A.C. were heard in the City, as for example, in the Lord Mayor's Waiting Book (which was a diary of the Lord Mayor's judicial activities) for 1663 is the following entry:

'Theis are to authorise and permitt the bearer thereof Capt. John Mordaunt to beat up Drums within the City of London towards the levyeing of forces for the foe in his Maty Service under the Command of the Earle of Teviott to Tangeire without any lett or molestacon. Giben under my hand this 8th of December, 1663.

Antho: Bateman'

Sir Anthony Bateman was Lord Mayor in 1663.

A year later there is an entry in the Lord Mayor's Waiting Book, dated September 21, 1664:

'This day likewise was granted by his Lordship to Sir Edward Broughton or to such officer as he shall appoint for the beating up of Drums in this Citty and Libertyes for fifty men Volunteers to go on ship board under the command of his highness Prince Rupert in his Matyes service . . . under the hand and seale of his Grace the Duke of Albemarle.'

The first recruiting of Marines (subsequently Royal Marines) in the City of London was in 1664. Application was made to the Lord Mayor, 'whereupon his Lordship graunted a license to the said Coll: Killigrew or any deputed by him to beat up Drumes within the Citty of London and Libties thereof for the purpose aforesaid.'

The aforesaid purpose was to raise The Admiral's Regiment, which was first mustered on November 16 of that year. Other entries in the Waiting Book also refer to the recruiting of Marines, as for example:

'October 30th, 1666. Theis are to authorize you by beat of Drum to raise such Voluntiers as you shall need not exceeding 100 men for the filling upp of your Company in his Royall Highness the Duke of York's Regiment under the command of Collonel Sir Christopher Wrey. And in case you shall beat upp yr Drums in the Cittye of London of the Libtie thereof you are first to acquaint the Lord Maior of London therewith. Given under my hand at the Cockpit the 26th of October, 1666.

Albemarle.'

'To Capt. Silius Titus
or such Officer as he shall appoint.'

The Royal Navy did its first recruiting in the City in 1668. It reads as follows:

'His Royall Highnesse haveing by his Warrt under his hand and Seale authorized and required Sir Robert Holmes Knt Capt. of his Mats Shipp the Defiace or his Order to beat uppe Drummes in such places as they should think fitt for the raiseing of Voluntier Seamen to serve on board the said shipp; upon request and viewe of the aforesaid Warrt his Lordship doth License and give leave that Drummes may bee beate within this Cittie and Libties for the purpose aforesaid . . . '

The peculiar position of the Honourable Artillery Company as an armed force in the City has never been disputed, nor its ancient right to its privileges. That it is emphatic on this point is shown in its own History, by G. Goold Walker, previously mentioned.

'Every year for upwards of 300 years, as its records show, it has marched through the City under arms, with drums beating, Colours flying, fifes and hautboys playing, and (since the introduction of that weapon) with bayonets fixed ... The tacit consent of the City to this practice in former years is understandable, since the Company was for centuries composed of citizens and freemen of London under the control of the City authorities, and when that connection ceased [with the formation of the Territorial Army], ancient usage had been established. Consequently it was surprising to find, when the question arose in 1924, that the archives of Guildhall furnished no official record of the privilege ever having been granted to the Company. The omission is probably accounted for by the fact that none had ever questioned our right in this matter. However, formal application to the Lord Mayor received favourable consideration, and the long-cherished privilege of the Company was officially placed on record.'

In 1768, when Parliament had been dissolved it was debated by the Court of Assistants of the H.A.C. 'whether it was eligible for this Company to go in a Body in their military uniform to vote for such gentlemen whom they should think proper to represent this City in Parliament.'

The outcome of it was that those members of the Company who were Liverymen and therefore had a Parliamentary vote, paraded at Armoury House and marched to Guildhall to register their votes, headed by a band of music.

Elegance has always been the mark of the Honourable Artillery Company, whether it be as pikemen immediately behind the Lord Mayor's coach, and on other Civic occasions, or when conducting their own social activities. When the first Regimental Ball took place in 1771, and then annually afterwards, it was laid down that 'each Member be particularly attentive to the Character of the Persons he introduces, as he will be considered responsible for their Conduct.' Another rule was that 'no Lady be admitted in an Undress'.

When the Company marched to Hyde Park in celebration of

the King's Birthday in 1782 they marched out of headquarters accompanied by two field pieces and baggage wagons. They were preceded by music playing, drums beating and Colours flying. The regimental band at the time consisted of four clarionets, two horns, one trumpet, and two bassoons. There was also a drum-major, eleven drummers and ten fifers.

The title of Drum-Major was first used in place of Drumbeater in 1692.

In the year 1794 the six regiments of City Trained Bands were regrouped in two regiments, the East and the West. Afterwards the Lieutenancy of the City, consisting of the Lord Mayor, the Aldermen, the Recorder, the Chamberlain, the Town Clerk, the Common Serjeant, the directors of the Bank of England, and others, applied for the use of the Artillery Ground and Armoury for the training of the reformed force. The Honourable Artillery Company were prepared to comply on certain conditions, but the Lieutenancy demanded the privilege as a right, which led to a legal struggle lasting for five years. At one stage the situation reached something approaching civil war! The two regiments were ordered to march to the Ground with drums beating and bayonets fixed to demand entrance. But when they got there the gates were locked and the Honourable Artillery Company drawn up within, ready to defend themselves against any attempt at forcible entry.

It was an embarrassing situation, solved by the two militia regiments marching away without a shot being fired!

One of the many colourful occasions in the history of the Company took place in the year 1684, when the Duke of York (afterwards James II) announced his intention of leading them in person on one of their General Marches:

'His Royall Highness having ordered the Artillery Company to march on Thursday the 26th of this Inst. June, And declared to honour the Company with hys Royall presence, you are therefore desired By the Court of Assistance To Appear in the Artillery

Garden by 9 of the Clock in the morning in your Compleatest arms and habbit with Red feather.'

After the Company had assembled and formed up it marched to the Lord Mayor's, 'where they were very Nobly Entertained,' and thence to Gracechurch Street, where they were paraded to receive the Duke of York, 'who came thither about Three o'Clock attended with a great many of the Nobility and other persons of quality divers of which carried arms in the Company. His Royal Highness was pleased to leave his Coach and march on Horseback at the Head of the Company . . . His Royal Highness's Troop of Horse Guards, and several of the Nobility and Persons of Quality on Horseback, marching before his Royal Highness.

'Being come to the Artillery-Ground his Royal Highness was pleased to quit his horse, and taking his Pike, lead the Body almost the length of the Ground. And here the Lord Mayor, the Aldermen and Sheriffs come in their Scarlette to pay their duty . . .

'Then his Royall Highness and Prince George [of Denmark] were entertained by Colonel Friend in his Tent at a very Noble and Splendid Banquet of Sweetmeats; Flutes, Hautboys and other Musick playing all the while . . . '

Thus once again honour is done to the sound of music, by what is undoubtedly the oldest unit in the British Army. In *The Book of Ceremonials of the City of London* are to be found these words:

'This is an ancient Company, and so far back as the Reign of Queen Elizabeth they were the Trainers of the Trained Bands of London.'

CHAPTER 10

THE CHARITY CHILDREN

When Haydn came to London in 1791 he was so moved during the Handel Festival held in Westminster Abbey that at the Hallelujah Chorus he burst into tears, exclaiming, 'He is master of us all!'

In 1792 he was again deeply affected. This was during the annual meeting of the charity children at St Paul's Cathedral, when 4,000 children sang a hymn composed by John Jones, organist of the cathedral. Afterwards he wrote in his diary 'No music has ever moved me so much in my life.'

The Charity Schools of London dated back to the earliest years of the eighteenth century, and for generation after generation the London Charity Schools attended the united annual service in St Paul's itself, usually in June.

Haydn's impression of the occasion was reflected by that of Hector Berlioz, who attended the service on June 5, 1851 with an invitation from John Goss, the Cathedral organist.

In a letter he wrote afterwards to a Paris newspaper he had this to say:

'I describe the unique impression made upon me lately in St Paul's Cathedral by the choir of 6,500 charity school children who meet there once a year. It is incomparably the most impressive, the most Babylonian ceremony at which up to now it has been my lot to attend.

'By ten o'clock the approaches to St Paul's were crowded with

128

John Banister, the first Concert Impresario. Born in
1630. Died in 1679

Thomas Britton, the Musical Small Coal Man. He
died in 1714

Renascentur quæ jam cecidere.

N. Dance inv.   F. Bartolozzi.

Early 19th Century
concert tickets. They
took many forms and
were of considerable
artistic merit

people and I had some difficulty in getting through . . .

'Nine almost vertical amphitheatres, 16 tiers high, had been put up for the children, under the dome and in the choir in front of the organ. The six under the dome formed a sort of hexagonal circus opening only east and west. From the latter opening stretched an inclined plane ending above the main entrance; it was already covered by a huge congregation.

' . . . To the left of the gallery, in front of the organ, there was a stand for 7 or 8 trumpets and drummers. On this stand a large mirror was placed so that the musicians might see the reflection of the choir-master beating time in the distance.

'Banners planted all round the vast amphitheatre – the sixteenth tier reached almost to the capitals of the columns marked the place of each school, and bore the names of the parishes and districts of London to which they belonged.

'As the children came in and filled the amphitheatre from top to bottom, the sight reminded me of the phenomenon of crystallization under a microscope . . . the dark blue of the boys on the top tiers, and the white of the girls on the lower. Further, as the boys had brass plates or silver medals on their jackets, these glittered as they moved like a thousand intermittent sparks on the dark background. The appearance of the girls' seats was still more curious, the green and pink ribbons worn by these little white maids, made their part of the amphitheatre look exactly like a snow-covered mountain with blades of grass and flowers peeping out here and there.

'Then there were the different hues among the congregation, the crimson throne of the Archbishop of Canterbury, the richly decorated benches of the Lord Mayor and the aristocracy, and high up at the other end the gilded pipes of the great organ . . .

'The magical effect was enhanced by the order, the quietitude and the serenity which reigned everywhere . . .

'After a chord on the organ, there burst forth in gigantic unison:

I

"All people that on earth do dwell
Sing to the Lord with cheerful voice . . . "

'It compares with the power and beauty of the finest vocal
masses you have ever heard . . . this hymn, with its broad notes
and sublime style, is supported by superb harmonies which the
organ gives out without drowning it.

' . . . When I heard the psalms in three-time by J. G. Anthony
an old English master (1774) sung by all the voices, with trumpets,
drums and the organ – a truly inspired composition with its grand
harmonies, my feelings overcame me, and I had to use my music
as Agamemnon did his toga, to hide my face . . .

'The children do not know music, they have never seen a note
in their lives. Every year for three months they are taught the
hymns and anthems for the Meeting, mechanically with the aid
of a violin. They learn them by heart.'

Berlioz' rapt wonder and emotion at the Annual Meeting of
the Charity Children is not reflected in *St Paul's in Its Glory*. The
author observes drily: 'The children attending them were
habituated from the first to being treated as a living advertisement
for the good works of which they enjoyed the benefit.'

At the Peace of Utrecht Queen Anne ordained that the
Thanksgiving Service should be held in St Paul's. Handel composed
his *Jubilate* and *Te Deum* specially for the occasion, and both
Houses of Parliament processed from Westminster to St Paul's.

In the Strand a great scaffold, more than 200 yards long and
composed of eight tiers of narrow seats were filled with 4,000
London Charity Children.

There they sang and repeated the hymns prepared for the
occasion to edify the Lords and Commons, and in expectation of
Queen. But as we know, the Queen never came. At the last
minute she decided to make her own thanksgiving in the Chapel
of St James's Palace.

The following year, when George I made his Royal Entry into

the City the London Charity Children were once more on parade – occupying a scaffold on the south side of St Paul's Churchyard, their childish voices raised in a hymn of praise.

The annual event of the Charity Children meeting in St Paul's continued until 1877. 'It normally took place in June, and it occupied the nave and the entire space beneath the dome; the Cathedral closed down regularly for a month in order to allow the erection of benches, tier above tier, for the children to occupy, blocking choir and transepts and reaching nearly half way up the piers of the arches; they were cramped for space, unable to kneel, and looked like exhibits in a flower show. The spirit in which the celebration had sometimes been conducted may be illustrated by the fact that in 1837 the service concluded with three cheers for the Lord Mayor!' (Extract from *St Paul's in Its Glory*).

1851, the year Hector Berlioz visited St Paul's, was also the year of the Great Exhibition of All Nations in Hyde Park. Berlioz had been sent by the French Government to be one of the judges of musical instruments submitted for awards.

The City of London had backed the project to the extent of nearly forty thousand pounds. The Lord Mayor, Aldermen and civic officers attended in state . . . Handel's Hallelujah Chorus, so we are told, 'thundered its powerful harmonies to the gratified ear'.

Hector Berlioz was, perhaps, not so emotionally impressed as he was to be a few days later at St Paul's. But after the grandeur of the Royal Opening of London's Great Exhibition, and the 'Babylonian' ceremony of the Charity Children, an odd little visit he made to the Crystal Palace early one morning, long before the doors were opened to the public but on production of his pass, made the perfect contrast.

'At seven in the morning the deserted interior of the palace of the Exhibition was a sight of peculiar grandeur – a vast solitude, no sound to break the silence, soft lights falling from the transparent roof, dry fountains, silent organs, motionless trees, a harmonious display of rich products brought from all corners of the earth by a hundred rival peoples. Ingenious works, the products of peace, instruments of destruction recalling war, all the causes of movement and noise appeared at the time to hold mysterious converse in the absence of man, in that unknown tongue which one hears with the ear of the spirit. I settled down to listen to their secret dialogue . . .

' . . . A noise not unlike the sound of rain was heard in the vast galleries; it was the jets of water and the fountains which the keepers had just set playing. The crystal castles, the artificial rocks, vibrated under the shower of liquid pearls. The policemen, the good unarmed "gendarmes" respected by everyone with so much reason, came to their posts . . . the diamonds, prudently hidden during the night, reappeared glittering in their cases.'

CHAPTER II

THE GUILDHALL SCHOOL OF MUSIC AND DRAMA

'The ancient custome of this honourable and renowned Citie hath been ever to retaine and maintaine excellent and expert Musicians.'

Those words were written by Thomas Morley, Organist at St Paul's Cathedral and Gentleman of the Chapel Royal in 1599. Morley, of his place and time, was a great musician, and his words have been a pride and inspiration in the City ever since. It is not surprising, therefore, that they have been adopted as the guiding principle of the Guildhall School of Music and Drama, administered as it is by the Music Committee of the Corporation of London.

It can be said with truth that the Guildhall School of Music and Drama is one of the famous music and drama schools of the world, and many musicians of subsequent fame learned their craft within its walls.

The list of such musicians and actors is imposing, both in its numbers and the stature of those who have brought lustre to this great City School. Dame Sybil Thorndyke, Carrie Tubb, Edna Best, Max Jaffa, Diana Churchill, William Primrose, C.B.E., Lilian Styles-Allen, Benjamin Frankel, Sidney Harrison, Dora Labette and Frand Lafitte, to name but a few who were students there and who have had the Fellowship of the Guildhall School of Music and Drama conferred upon them for their distinguished professional work.

Holders of the Gold Medal include such names as William Primrose, Walter Nunn, Sidney Harrison, Sidney Bowman, Joshua Glazier, Pauline Sadgrove, Leonard Friedman and Jacqueline du Pre as Instrumentalists. Among the Gold Medalists who are singers are Esther Coleman, Martin Boddey, Margaret Tann Williams, Norman Walker, Gwen Catley, David Lloyd, Rose Hill, Owen Brannigan, Pamela Woolmore, Richard Standen, Iona Jones and Benjamin Luxton.

The Guildhall School of Music was founded in 1880. The idea of such a school being nurtured in the City is considerably older. Many years before the School's foundation two progressive and liberal-minded members of the Common Council, Mr John Cox and Mr John Bath, had been agitating for recognition on the part of the Corporation of the necessity of teaching music to those of its citizens who desired it.

It was at the time advanced and enlightened thinking. Music at that point in English history was not a fashionable recreation, and was at a low ebb. Many Victorian male parents, products of a hard-headed business age, had a robust John Bull prejudice against music being part of the curriculum of their children's education.

Such views as this, however, were undergoing some stress, and found increasingly difficult to substantiate, consequent on the way events had turned in Europe. In 1871 the French were decisively defeated by a nation which was admitted to be the most musical, and now showing itself to be the most efficient and military and muscular!

The ground was indeed shifting, not to mention the work of Sir George Grove and Arthur Sullivan, and the Saturday Concerts conducted by August Manns at the Crystal Palace.

In 1875 the Prince of Wales wrote to the Lord Mayor of London, inviting his support and that of the Corporation in the founding of a National Training School for Music at South Kensington.

At that time the only institution of its kind was the Royal

Academy of Music, which had been founded in 1822, but by now there was definitely the need for a second school of music, such as was envisaged in the proposed National Training School of Music.

The City immediately supported the Prince's plan, produced their share of money for the project, and appointed a Music Deputation to look after their interests in the matter.

But for various reasons the National Training School, despite its influential support, never really got off the ground, and in 1882 it was remoulded on new lines as the Royal College of Music, taking over the valuable assets of the former National Training School for Music.

Meanwhile, an event took place in the City which was to have far-reaching effects. In January, 1879, a Mr Weist Hill started the Guildhall Orchestral Society and Choir, an amateur body which gave occasional performances in Guildhall and elsewhere.

Various members of the Common Council who felt strongly that the City should have its own centre of musical instruction continued to press their views, while a few of the more reactionary Councilmen threw cold water on the idea.

The pro-music group won their point, and the Music Deputation, though they had their hands full with the then limping National Training School, were requested 'to consider if there be any demand for musical education in the City of London, such as exists in the West End of London, and the best mode for supplying such education.'

The request was made June 19, 1879, and the Music Deputation gave a full report of their findings in the following March.

They fully supported the idea. They had no doubt whatsoever that a demand for musical education existed in the City. The establishment of the Guildhall Orchestral Society and Choir under Mr Weist Hill was an indication of that. On all sides they had found persons 'desirous to attain in a higher degree the knowledge and exercise of the practice and principles of musical science, so as to execute well, and to comprehend fully, the works of the great masters.'

In this summing up, it may be noted, an important departure was being made from that of the long established Royal Academy of Music and the recently launched National Training School for Music, of which Arthur Sullivan had been made first Principal. Whereas they had been established to train professional musicians, the proposed City school, while also doing that, should open its doors to amateur musicians and teach them how to 'execute well and comprehend fully' classical and other masterpieces, and thus increase audiences.

The Music Deputation pointed out that good musical education in London had been very costly, 'and the result had been that many persons are employed in teaching, who may have some facility in the exercise of the manual part of that so-called profession, but little, if any, in the fundamental principles of the art they profess to teach.'

The Deputation envisaged a school of music in the City, backed by the Corporation, and easily accessible to students as would make redundant the half-competent suburban teachers who gave eight to twelve lessons at the homes of their pupils for a guinea. If the new school were established, thoroughly qualified professors had agreed to co-operate at a very low price per pupil. By being daily at the school the teacher would be on the spot, and his pupils would come to him. Thus he would not lose time and extra travelling costs in driving from house to house giving lessons. Nor would he contract bad debts! He could give tuition at a central institution at half the price he would be compelled to charge for private lessons.

On this basis it was estimated that a few of the professors would earn £1,000 a year, while others would earn £500 and upwards.

The report was accepted by the Common Council, and granted £350 as a beginning towards the establishment of the school, and lent nine rooms in an empty wool warehouse in

Aldermanbury, hard by Guildhall, as temporary premises.

In such a modest way as this the Guildhall School of Music started in September 1880, with 62 pupils. Mr Weist Hill was appointed the first Principal.

The success of the school was immediate. By the end of the first year the school had gathered to itself 216 pupils and 29 professors, and by the end of 1881 there were 907 students and 58 professors.

In the space of those two short active years the Guildhall School of Music had grown far beyond Mr Weist Hill's most optimistic anticipation. It had also become too unwieldy for the Music Deputation, who had been given the task, to manage it. The Court of Common Council appointed a Ward Committee to take its place. This new Management Committee was composed of one or more members selected from each of the Wards of the City.

At the end of 1882 the Guildhall School had 1,430 students and 75 professors. Two years after that there were 2,314 students and 82 professors.

By that time the converted wool warehouse had become impossibly small and inconvenient. Classrooms had been sub-divided by thin lath and plaster walls with glass partitions at the top. The students were treading on each other's toes.

A contemporary account has this to say: 'The Babel of sound was simply deafening, and it often keenly aroused the ire of some of the foreign teachers. Rehearsals had to be held at the City of London School, organ lessons were given at the church in Aldermanbury, and an unfortunate gentleman student of a trombone was chased from room to room.

New premises would have to be found, and in July, 1884, despite opposition, a Committee was appointed by the Common Council to consider details. In March 1885 the Committee reported in favour of the present site in John Carpenter Street just off the Victoria Embankment by Blackfriars.

The site was adopted, the City Corporation voting £20,000 cash for the building, and the school to pay £1,000 a year ground rent. The Foundation Stone was laid in 1885, and by the end of 1886 the building was ready to receive students. The original plan had been to use Bath stone for the outside of the building, but this was subsequently changed to Portland stone, as being considered more suitable. The effect of the change was to put up the cost by between £5,000 and £6,000.

The new building contained 45 classrooms. A system was worked out at almost conveyor-belt level whereby 135 lessons, each lasting an hour, could be given in one hour. The method was intensive, but that was because the need was there. In practice each student received twenty minutes of individual tuition to be followed by remaining in the room to attend to the instruction given to the two following students.

Each classroom was furnished with a grand piano, and sometimes with an upright one in addition. On the second floor was a large room possessing a complete stage for presenting opera, and accommodating an audience of over 200 people.

The Graphic of January 12, 1889 carries the information that in respect to the classrooms 'the upper half of the double doors opening on to the corridors is made of glass, this device being adopted partly as a protection to the professors against hysterical girls, partly to reassure naturally anxious parents!'

Mr Weist Hill died in 1891, and was succeeded as Principal by the great choral conductor and composer, Sir Joseph Barnby, who added further classrooms and a well-appointed theatre.

In an article to *The Strand Musical Magazine*, Volume 1, 1895, Sir Joseph Barnby has this to say:

'Every branch of music is taught . . . French, German and Italian languages, gesture, deportment and elocution.

'Professors will bear comparison with that of any other school in existence. It is only necessary to mention such names as Sims Reeves, Gustave Garcia, Albert Visetti, Wilhelm Ganz, Herman

Klein, Edwin Holland, Frederick Walker, Ernst Pauer, Benno Schonberger, John F. Barnett, Ridley Prentice, J. Baptist Calkin, E. Silas, Francesco Berger, Professor Wilhelmj, Johannes Wilff, Alfred Gibson, B. Hollander, Ernest de Munck . . .

'It will be noted that perhaps the most characteristic feature of the institution is embodied in the statement that, whilst the majority of the great music schools in this country devote their energies to the training of professional musicians, the Guildhall School of Music offers its advantages equally to those who are likely to form our future audiences. The benefit resulting from this spread of musical knowledge amongst amateurs will not be far to seek. The young people of today will be the heads of families in the next generation, and they will not only be able to enjoy music with a more intelligent and cultivated mind themselves, but in turn will be able to exercise greater discrimination in the selection of teachers, and in deciding on the course of study of their children.'

Concerning the work in the Guildhall School of Music at that time, Sir Joseph Barnby drew a clear picture.

'Every fortnight students cross the road to the magnificent hall of the City of London School, and there give concerts of a miscellaneous character.

'Short of possessing a great Concert Hall of their own, nothing could be much more satisfactory than the hall of the City of London School. Led up to by a marble staircase that would glorify a palace, the room itself is still sufficiently stately and beautiful to astonish anyone who sees it for the first time. Of a size sufficiently great to accommodate an audience of 1,700 people "on the flat" . . . in this hall may be heard the most promising students of the institution, in consideration of whom, the concerts take place at the unusual time of 6.30 p.m., lasting an hour and a half.

'Not the least interesting function for a stranger to attend is the weekly orchestral rehearsal, conducted by the Principal, in which over 100 students – mostly female – take part. Here they are taken through the Symphonies of Beethoven, Mendelssohn, Schumann, Brahms, and other composers. On Thursday evenings the Orchestra is replaced by a choir numbering over 200 voices. Again, on Saturday afternoons the practice room is occupied by the Opera class, where the young "principals" are rehearsed for the various operatic performances, the floor of the room being marked to correspond with the dimensions of the London theatre where the performance is intended to take place.'

Nearly 6,000 lessons were being given each week at the Guildhall School of Music in 1895 – a fantastic achievement in an institution at that time only fifteen years old.

Early in the history of the School the necessity for Exhibitions became apparent. One girl student used to bring her money in every imaginable form from shillings down to farthings. At length there was no money, and this promising young artist was in danger of being obliged to give up.

But the girl's attempts to pay for her tuition did not pass unnoticed, and it came to the ears of an Alderman who put down the whole of the money necessary. The girl was able to complete her course and embark on a promising professional career.

It was following this that the City Corporation made arrangements to contribute £200 a year, thereby enabling forty students to be wholly or partially taught out of that amount. The Salters' Company followed suit and gave 20 guineas a year, and the Merchant Taylors £20 a year. The Worshipful Company of Musicians gave particular attention and help to the School in the matter of Exhibitions.

Today there are an important number of scholarships awarded to outstanding candidates at the annual entrance auditions and, secondly, as the result of competition amongst internal students. The list is considerable, as is the list of annual prizes to be won by students who have completed three terms at the school.

CHAPTER 12

THE WHITE SWAN OF APOLLO

Fiftieth in the order of precedence of the Guilds of the City of London, the Worshipful Company of Musicians, with its Master, Wardens, Court, its members of the Livery and its Freemen, its Laws and Orders, is the direct and lineal descendent of those earlier working guilds and fellowships of musicians and minstrels residing in the City. Its chequered history includes those long-ago skirmishes with the King's Musicians, who all but destroyed it in their fratricidal warfare.

Those struggles were basically a matter of survival in a ruthless age. The wandering minstrels, the 'foreigners' who were for ever gravitating to the City like pilgrims to some Mecca, and competing against the native talent for the favours of a fickle public, made necessary the rules and regulations that would offer some stability for the London-bred musicians. The skill of the City musician was not sufficient in itself. He needed also, as was so exactly laid down in the ritual words of another and remote guild, the Ancient Order of Scottish Wheelwrights, 'Counsel, support, and above all protection.' The Guild of Minstrels of London sought that thing, but it required the added weight and strength of the City to impart durability.

As we know, the Society of Minstrels of the City of London forfeited its Charter of James I, and one cannot deny the fact that the then 'Master, Wardens and Commonalty of the Art of Science of the Musicians of London' had been skating on very

The Arms of the Worshipful Company of Musicians

Azure within a double tressure flory counterflory Or a Swan rousant Argent, on a chief Gules a Pale between two Lions passant guardant of the second thereon a Rose of the fourth barbed vert and seeded gold.

thin ice before they got their ducking. But the inherent durability remained, the Order survived, and in the fullness of time, on December 29, 1950 the Royal Charter of King George VI replaced the Charter which had been lost.

In its time it had been a hard-working City Guild, endeavouring to obtain some sort of security for its musician members in what has always been a notoriously precarious profession. Burney's acid comment, that 'this company has ever been held in derision by real professors, who have regarded it as an intrusion as foreign to the cultivation and prosperity of Good Music as the train-bands to the art of war', carries no validity with respect to the Worshipful Company of Musicians or, for that matter, to the Honourable Artillery Company. Likewise, Hawkins' derisive 'the honourable fraternity of Musicians of the City of London derive the sole and exclusive privilege of fiddling and trumpeting to the mayor and aldermen and of scrambling for the fragments of a city feast', is a sheer distortion of fact.

But what, one may ask, is the standing of the Worshipful Company of Musicians of London today? Has it any real relationship with the musical profession, or is it merely a theoretical and dilettante anachronism?

The Company's own records indeed suggest that this was the case during the eighteenth century. At the beginning of that century its strength was a mere nineteen members. Ninety-four years later it had increased to 264.

'This great accretion in strength,' says Brigadier H. A. F. Crewdson, Clerk to the Company (1930–67), 'was rather brought about by social conditions than by any great renaissance of interest in Music. Even before the opening of the century, that westward movement of the cultural centres of London had begun which was ultimately to leave the City nothing but a tiny handful of its formerly teeming Artists and Craftsmen . . .

'With the election, however, to the Court in 1870 of William Chappell, Musician and Antiquarian, the seeds were sown of a new order. Chappell revivified the Company by interesting in it a number of his musical friends, and though he did not live to see the result, his infusion of new blood into the Company had far-reaching consequences for its welfare.

'At long last the Guild re-focussed its attention upon the Art to which it was dedicated. The admission to the Court of Bridge (Sir John Frederick Bridge, Master 1892 and 1898 at which period he held the appointments of Organist, Westminster Abbey, and Gresham Professor of Music) in 1885, and Sir John Stainer, appointed Professor of Music at Oxford, 1889, a few years later, was an earnest of the new outlook.'

The wider activities of the Company in the field of music in the last eighty years make in themselves an illuminating answer as to the true quality of its existence. The list of its interests in contributing to the furtherance of music, both in the City and outside, is a formidable one, and must be accepted as a classic example of the practical value today of a City Company promoting its own mistery.

The Guildhall School of Music was founded in 1880. In 1889 the Musicians Company instituted the Company's Silver Medal to be awarded triennially at the Royal Academy of Music, the Royal College of Music, and the Guildhall School of Music in rotation, the Award being made to the most distinguished student of the year, nominated without competition or examination by the Head of the Institution concerned, assisted by two of his principal professors. The cost of the medals were to be defrayed out of the Company's General Fund.

In 1956, consequent on the gift to the Company of the Lady Corbett Memorial Fund, followed by that of the Bannerman-Lockett Fund, the Company was enabled to grant the Silver Medal annually to those three great schools of music. The joint operation of the Corbett and Bannerman-Lockett funds resulted in the cost of the Medal awarded to students of the Guildhall School of Music and Drama becoming an annual charge upon the

Music in a private house by Marcellus Laroon

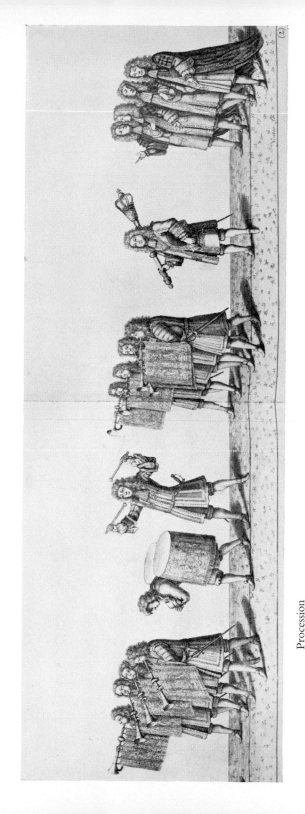

Procession

Taken from the History of the Coronation of James II, printed by Thomas Newcombe, one of His Majesty's Printers, 1687. The whole work is illustrated by several 'sculptures' (engravings,) of which this illustration is part. The artist was Nicholas Yeates, and the illustration shows trumpets and kettle-drums as an item of the Coronation Procession.

In the History is the description '. . . the Drums Beat a March and the Trumpets sounded several Levets, and the Choirs sang all the way.'

Company's funds instead of triennial as before. In 1959, however, a gift from Mr H. Seymour Fowler, a Liveryman of the Company endowed the Medal for the Guildhall School in the same way as the others.

In 1893 a sum of £9 9s was presented annually out of the Company's General Fund to the Guildhall School of Music, to be competed for by Students of Composition. Then in the year 1904 a gift to the Company by the late Mr Andrew Carnegie enabled them to found two Scholarships at the Guildhall School of Music, each entitling the holder to three years' free tuition. A special condition of the award was that candidates should show marked ability in Sight Reading. It is sad to have to relate that in the face of rising costs, which necessitated an increase in the fees at the Guildhall School, in 1925 the two Scholarships were reluctantly merged into one.

On August 1, 1901, the Master, Wardens and Court offered a prize of Fifty Guineas together with the Freedom and Livery of the Company for the composition of an Orchestral March, suitable for performance at the time of King Edward VII's Coronation. The prize was won by Mr Percy Godfrey, Mus.Bac., Master of Music at King's School, Canterbury. The March was played at the Coronation on August 9, 1902, and was published. The Royalties amounted to £866, and were given to King Edward's Hospital Fund. The composer, Mr Godfrey, was duly admitted to the Freedom and Livery, and lived to become one of the Company's most senior members.

The Company's work and sense of its responsibility towards the furtherance of music was gathering impetus with the turn of the century. A Court was held on January 20, 1903, when it was unanimously resolved that the three hundredth anniversary of the granting by King James I of a Charter of Incorporation of the Musicians' Company on the 8th day of July, 1604, be celebrated by holding an Exhibition of Ancient Musical Instruments, Manuscripts, Autographs, Portraits, Books and other mementoes of music and musicians, under the auspices of the Company.

(It would seem that at that time, and the years previously, a veil had been drawn over the unhappy circumstances of the revocation of the Charter!)

The patronage of King Edward, Queen Alexandra, and the Prince and Princess of Wales was graciously given to the Exhibition, while the Worshipful Company of Fishmongers granted the use of their magnificent Hall by London Bridge for staging the Exhibition for a period of four weeks. The Fishmongers also bore the greater portion of the cost of the magnificent opening ceremony, which was performed by the Prince and Princess of Wales.

The Exhibition included a rare range of historic instruments, manuscripts and mementoes, and surpassed in completeness any other that had been hitherto held. Important lectures were delivered daily by eminent authorities.

This resurgence of Guild activities became an increasingly marked feature of the Musicians' Company in the twentieth century. A beautifying of the Company's Latin Grace:

'Oculi omnium in Te sperant, et Tu das escam
illorum in tempore opportuno. Gloria Tibi, Domine.
Amen.'

was sought by offering a money prize for the best musical setting. That was in the year 1904, and is known as the Crews' Prize. It was won by the late Charles Wood, M.A., Mus.D., of Gonville and Caius College, Cambridge. It gave the Company a sung Grace of exquisite beauty, which is sung before all important Dinners. An additional prize was given by Mr Crews for another setting of the Grace by Mr Arthur Henry Brown.

In 1905 the Cobbett Prize Competition for £50 was offered for the best composition of a Phantasy String Quartet. The form was to be in the style of the old English 'Fancy', as, for example, those of Thomas Weelkes, Richard Deering and Orlando Gibbons, described in Chapter 4, and was intended to popularise the old form of 'Fancy'. Subsequently two other prizes were added by

Mr Edward Ernest Cooper (later Sir Ernest Cooper, Lord Mayor of London) and Mr H. L. Sternberg.

The impetus of the Worshipful Company of Musicians was growing. In 1905 Mr Ernest Palmer, later to become the Rt Hon. Lord Palmer of Reading, gave the Company £1,000, which with his agreement was devoted to the establishment of two Scholarships at the Guildhall School of Music. In the next year he added £250 to his gift. As with the previous scholarships mentioned, time came when, in consequence of rising costs, the two scholarships had to be merged into one, which was done in the year 1926.

It was the wish of the Donor of this Scholarship that it should be held by an ex-chorister of St Paul's Cathedral or Westminster Abbey. Failing a candidate from those sources, it was to be awarded to a girl under 18 years of age. The Scholarship is for two years' tuition, with an extension to a third year in cases of special merit.

A fund was raised within the Livery of the Company in the year 1907, and was dedicated to the memory of the late Leopold Lawrence Stern, the distinguished violoncellist. It took the name, The Leo Stern Memorial Gift, 1907, and its purpose was to award a sum of Five Guineas each year to a poor Student of the violoncello at the Royal College of Music, the Student to be selected by the Director. The late Past Master of the Musicians' Company, Mr A. F. Hill, distinguished as a historian of the Company, was the prime mover of this prize, the capital sum of which was raised entirely within the ranks of the Company.

In the year 1908 the Company's Silver Medal was extended in its scope of influence. It was decided to present it annually to the Royal Military School of Music, and, in 1910, annually to the Royal Naval School of Music. The cost of the latter medal was provided from an endowment given to the Company by the late Mr Hugh Wyatt – he became Master in 1918 – for that purpose. In 1955 the Court decided that the Silver Medal should also be awarded annually to the Royal Air Force School of Music.

Miss Alice Margaret Dalrymple Prendergast presented, in 1913, £500 to the Company in memory of her late brother, Mr Arthur Hugh Dalrymple Prendergast, M.A., who had been elected an Honorary Freeman of the Company. The intention behind this fund was to obtain apprenticeships for Choir Boys of the Parish Churches of the Church of England within the area of the City of London, excepting St Paul's Cathedral. Having received the consent of Miss Prendergast, the Court decided to allow the income of the Fund to accumulate for some years and be added to the capital in order to increase the Fund.

At the end of the 1914–18 war a new factor arose. There was no City church still employing choir boys. It was therefore decided by the Court in 1950 to put into effect the secondary object of the scheme for the Fund, and to give the income of the Fund, amounting to about £45 annually, to the Principal of the Royal Academy of Music, for the benefit of a deserving student, at his discretion.

In the year 1924 the Walter Willson Cobbett Medal was instituted, to be presented annually to distinguished musicians for services to the Art of Chamber Music, and was first presented to Thomas Frederick Dunhill. The award is considered among musicians to be an important one, and is highly rated. At one time the specially designed medal was struck in gold, but it is now, inevitably, in silver gilt. Among the many famous recipients of the Medal are Sir Edward Elgar, Frank Bridge, Ralph Vaughan Williams, Dame Myra Hess, and Yehudi Menuhin. In 1933 it was awarded posthumously to Charles Wood.

Possibly the most important of the Company's contributions to the furtherance of the Art of Music lies in the John Clementi Collard Fellowship, 1931. The Company benefited by the will of John Clementi Collard, who died in 1918, to the extent of over £8,500. Absolutely no conditions were attached to the gift, but after very careful deliberation the Master, Wardens and Court determined to set the whole fund aside for the purpose of endowing a Fellowship to be called the John Clementi Collard Fellowship in Music.

The Fellowship is open to any British-born musician over the age of 27 years and under the age of 50. It is designed to give practical assistance, for a period not exceeding three years, to a musician of proved ability, who is prevented as a result of financial stringency, from employing his talents to their fullest extent. The Fellowship, which is a free gift from the Company, carries with it an honorarium of £400 free from deductions in the first year and a similar sum in each subsequent year of the Fellowship until termination.

To qualify for the Fellowship the candidate must have shown undoubted excellence in one or more of the higher branches of musical activity.

In 1935 the Court resolved that the first and every subsequent Fellow should upon the expiration of his Fellowship be admitted to the Freedom and Livery of the Company, the Fellowship fund defraying the fines and fees, as well as the fee payable to the City Chamberlain's Office for taking up the Freedom of the City.

The Cassel Prizes, 1946, are prizes presented annually to the Royal Marines School of Music, the Royal Military School of Music, and the Royal Air Force School of Music. The prizes take the form of a Silver and Bronze Medal at each School, the Medals being presented to Junior Musicians at the Royal Marines School, and to pupil Students at the Royal Military School.

The Royal Air Force prizes in this category were in limbo until a School of Music was established in that Service, and were first presented in 1952. To the accumulation of income which had resulted from this delayed commencement of awards, Sir Felix Cassel made a further gift in augmentation and the Cassel Silver Challenge Bowl was presented for competition between Bands of the Royal Air Force, excluding the Central Band. This

Bowl is the object of keen annual competition, and the standard demanded of the winning band each year is extremely high.

A Fund which had been donated to the Company by Mr J. H. Iles, O.B.E., Master of the Company in 1932, was divided at the request of Mr Iles, a large part of the Fund being given to the Bandsmen's National Memorial Fund, and the remaining portion retained in hand by the Company, which is now applied for the presentation annually of the Company's Silver Medal to an individual noted for service to the Brass Band movement.

The Mary Naomi Wallace Medal is presented annually to a recommended member of the W.R.A.C. Band. The Arthur Bulgin Medal is presented each year to an outstanding member of the National Youth Orchestra. The H.A.F. Crewdson Fund is for annual prizes at the Household Brigade Junior Musicians Wing.

Upon the formation of the 10th Battalion Royal Fusiliers (City of London Regiment) in September 1914, the Musicians' Company presented the Band Instruments, and in 1916 presented Gold Watches to five Bandsmen who had won the Victoria Cross. During the Great War of 1939–45 the Company gave an annual sum to charities for distressed musicians. This sum was equivalent to the Company's saving on Banquets and other meetings suspended during hostilities.

It is in such expressions as these, and in an age very different from the one in which the Company first came into being, that the Worshipful Company of Musicians of London shows a good and practical reason for its continued existence.

In 1914, Mr Claudius J. Ash, a Liveryman of the Company, suggested that a Benevolent Fund should be started, and gave a lead by contributing £500. The Fund was inaugurated for assisting distressed Musicians, preference being given to those who might have been connected with the Company in any way – as Liverymen, Scholarship Holders, Medallists, etc. The annual income of the Fund is administered by the Court.

In the service of music for its own sake, the late Mr Clifford Blackburn Edgar, who was master of the Company in 1913, bequeathed £1,000, the income of which was to be spent on providing additional music at the Company's annual celebration of St Cecilia's Day, or in the revival of English Classical Music at the General Livery Dinners of the Company, or partly for both occasions.

Another Past Master of the Company, the late Mr Walter Willson Cobbett bequeathed to the Company in 1937 the sum of £100 to be applied in amplifying the programme of music played after the Dinners given by the Company.

It can be said with truth that the fiftieth in the line of seniority of the City Guilds, while sharing in the general renaissance which has been enjoyed by all the Companies during the present century, has both enriched the City of London and itself by its devotion to the Art and Science of Music from which it sprang. The humble nature of the poor City minstrel or musician of the middle ages, so different in his status and way of life from the prosperous merchants, yet sustained his Guild despite the slings and arrows of the outrageous fortune he so often suffered. The present status of the Worshipful Company of Musicians, and the command it has in the affairs that concern it, more than justify – and account for – a survival against odds that might well have defeated a lesser Fellowship.

The Arms of the Company, granted by Camden, in 1604, and approved by Sir Henry St George Richmond in 1632, show on Azure within a double tressure flory counterflory Or a Swan rousant Argent. Should anyone think that device alludes to the mournful notes of the dying swan he would be in error. The swan there represented is the snow white and musical swan of Apollo, son of Zeus, and whose lyre forms the Crest above the Coat of Arms.

Let the Livery Flourish!

CHAPTER 13

THE MERRY BELLS

'Oranges and lemons,' say the bells of St Clement's.
'You owe me five farthings,' say the bells of St Martin's.
'When will you pay me?' say the bells of Old Bailey.
'When I grow rich,' say the bells of Shoreditch.
'When will that be?' say the bells of Stepney.
'I do not know,' says the great bell of Bow.

The bells of London make a merry kind of music, like nowhere else. By the sound of them alone a man would know he was in London. Though Big Ben half a mile up river in Westminster is probably the most instantaneously recognisable of all bells, nevertheless the largest in Britain, and the most dramatic, is Great Paul.

Great Paul is the most majestic of all the Passing Bells in the land. From the Home Secretary to the Lord Mayor: 'I have to request your Lordship will give directions for tolling the Great Bell of St Paul's Cathedral.' With leather-muffled clapper it tolls the passing of the great in the land from where it hangs in the southern tower of St Paul's.

Indeed, the ringing of the Passing Bell is one of the oldest acts of bellringing in English Christianity. In early times it was devoutly believed that demons were banished by the sound of a bell, and a departing soul would be in the greatest need of this help.

In the *Golden Legend* Wynkyn de Worde has this to say:

'It is said ye evil spirytes that ben in ye region of ye ayre doubte moche whan they here the belles ringen; and this is ye cause why the belles ringen whan it Thundreth, and whan grete tempeste and rages of wether happen, to ye ende that ye feinds and wycked spirytes should ben abashed and flee and cease of ye movynge of tempest.'

Latimer, who was later to die at the stake for the fervour of his convictions, derided this aspect of demonology when he preached a sermon in 1552.

'See here the foolishness of people, that in the time of the light of God's most holy word will follow such phantasies and delusions of the devil! Ye know, when there was a storm of fearful weather, then we rang the holy bells; they were they that must make all things well; they must drive away the devil! But I tell you, if the holy bells would serve against the devil, or that he might be put away through their sound, no doubt we would soon banish him out of all England. For, I think, if all the bells in England should be rung together at a certain hour, I think there would be almost no place, but some bells might be heard there. And so the devil should have no abiding place in England, if ringing of bells should serve; but it is not that will serve against the devil.'

In 1873 St Paul's possessed very few bells. There were two to strike the quarter chimes, and a large bell to ring the hours and for tolling. There was a small bell in the north-west to call Londoners to worship.

It was in that year that the Chapter resolved that such poverty of bells in a great cathedral should be remedied. Money was raised to install a carillon for the south-west tower. A peal of twelve bells was hung in the north-west tower, being the gift of the Corporation of the City and various of the Livery Companies. The Corporation's gift was the tenor bell of the peal. It weighs 3 tons 2 cwt. The bells were dedicated by Bishop Jackson after Evensong on All Saints' Day, 1878.

The late Revd. G. L. Prestige, D.D., formerly Canon and Treasurer of St Paul's, in his history of the Cathedral, *St Paul's in*

Its Glory, records that the first 'scientific' peal of the new bells was rung by the Society of College Youths in 1881. The peal lasted 4 hours and 17 minutes, and the devoted and experienced ringers were locked in the ringing chamber until it was finished.

It has been computed that with twelve bells there are nearly 480 million 'changes', and to ring them all would take more than thirty-three years continual bellringing!

In 1881 the Great Bell was ordered, and it came to St Paul's in the following May. Great Paul weighs 16 tons 14 cwt 75 lb. It has a diameter of 9 feet 6¾ inches. The note is E Flat.

It had first been intended to hang the bell in the north-west tower, but a re-examination of the factors involved revealed serious objections to hoisting the enormous bell to a position above the existing peal. Furthermore, there would be structural dangers in swinging it at such an elevation. The great bell's destination was therefore transferred to the southern tower.

It was a complicated and delicate operation. The bell was brought by a massive truck to within fifty feet of the chosen tower, and from there was drawn on a specially laid platform to the base of the tower. The actual method of raising was devised by the Royal Engineers, who used powerful lifting gear borrowed from Ordnance. It took three days to hoist the bell to where it now hangs in a great cage of timber that rests on a ledge in the masonry.

The bell bears the inscription *vae mihi si non evangelizavero*, which is taken from 1 Corinthians 9. 16: 'Woe is unto me, if I preach not the gospel.' Orders were given that Great Paul should bear its witness by being chimed every weekday for five minutes from one o'clock.

Among the many churches that were destroyed in the Great Fire of London in 1666, there were four churches related by proximity to each other. They were All Hallows', Lombard Street, St Benet's, Gracechurch Street, St Leonard's, Eastcheap, and St Dionis', Backchurch.

All Hallows' was rebuilt in 1694.

St Benet's was rebuilt in 1685.

St Leonard's was not rebuilt, and its parish was merged with that of St Benet's.

St Dionis' was rebuilt in 1674, and a hundred foot high tower was added ten years later. A ring of ten bells were purchased in 1727 at a cost of £479 18s.

St Benet's was pulled down in 1867, and the combined parish of St Benet's and St Leonard's were merged with that of All Hallows'.

In 1868 St Dionis' was also demolished. Its parish was added to that of All Hallows', and the ring of bells were re-hung in the tower of All Hallows'.

In 1938–39 the Church of All Hallows', Lombard Street, was taken down stone by stone, and the City thereby lost another of her daughters. But not as she had lost St Benet's, St Leonard's, and St Dionis, Backchurch, where Dr Burney had been organist, and of which Pepys wrote in his Diary 'very great store of fine women there in this church, more than I know anywhere about us.'

All Hallows' was rebuilt at Twickenham, and, such was the meticulous care, every memorial and gravestone within the fabric went as well. Today All Hallows', Twickenham, described as the 'successor' church, is like a piece of the City of London in exile, so impregnated with the City is its every stone. It gives one a curious feeling to read in the worn stone at one's feet: 'Beneath this spot lies . . . '. Close by is a memorial tablet with the words, 'Near this spot lies . . . ', when in fact the remembered dust lies in the City twenty miles to the east.

Perhaps one of the stranger aspects of this strange history, in which so much was lost or given away, is that All Hallows' should have retained the peal of ten bells that once sounded in the City, bequeathed to it when St Dionis' was demolished.

All Hallows' in its turn, when its stones came down in the City, offered its ring of bells to the new Guildford Cathedral.

The tenor bell weighs 19 cwt. Eight of the bells are by Thomas Lester, 1750, and the others by Richard Phelps, 1726.

But Guildford Cathedral declined the offered gift as not having a heavy enough ring. So the bells were successfully re-hung in All Hallows', Twickenham, in 1951, which, short of their sound being heard in the City, is no doubt the best place for them.

In the London records the early craftsmen who made bells called themselves potters. An agreement with the Prior of the Convent of the Church of Holy Trinity in London, in the year 1312 is given in Riley's *Memorials of London Life*. The spelling is given in modern English.

'Richard de Wymbissh, potter and citizen of London, came here before the Chamberlain on the Friday next after the Feast of St Mark the Evangelist, in the fifth year of the reign of King Edward, son of King Edward, and acknowledged that he was bound to Sir Ralph, Prior of the Church of the Holy Trinity in London, and the Convent of that place, to make one bell, good, entire, and well-sounding, as nearly in tune, to the utmost of his power, with the greater bell of the church aforesaid. And the said bell was to weigh 2,820 pounds, of good and befitting metal, every hundredweight thereof containing 112 pounds; the same to be ready for the Feast known as St Peter's Chains, next ensuing without any further delay. And should he not do so, then he agreed, &c., as proved by his recognizance.

'The same Prior also agreed to redeliver unto the said Richard the great bell which he had formerly made for the use of him and his Convent; and that without delay, so soon as the same Richard should commence founding the bell aforesaid, upon view thereof by the present threat. Afterwards, Alan de Middletone, Canon and Sacrist of the said house, came and acknowledged that the said Richard had fully satisfied them as to the work aforesaid; and therefore this recognizance was cancelled.'

Richard de Wymbissh did not contract to make the new bell exactly in tune with the old one, which suggests that the skill in bell-founding had not reached the precision it later attained.

The old church of St Michael Royal on College Hill possessed in the seventeenth century a ring of six bells, on which the young gentlemen of the neighbourhood used to amuse themselves by chiming in rounds. The following is taken from the Rule Book of the Ancient Society of College Youths, as published in the *History and Art of Change Ringing* by E. Morris.

'On the 5th of November, 1637 Lord Brereton, Sir Cliff Clifton, the Marquis of Salisbury, Lord Dacre, some of the City Aldermen, and many of the gentlemen in the vicinity of the College, founded the Society of College Youths, for the purpose of practising and promoting the art of ringing. For some time after the formation of the Company rounds and call changes were rung, but at length the Society achieved 120 changes of Bob Doubles on five bells, and it is supposed to be about 1642 when changes were first rung. Little progress was made till about 1677, when Mr Fabian Stedman, a printer, and a native of Cambridge, and who may be called the "father" of change-ringing, published his *Campanalogia*, dedicating it to the "Noble Society of College Youths", of which he was one of the most honoured members. About this time Stedman's method was first rung at St Benet's, Cambridge, by the College Youths, who paid a visit to that town.'

Shipway, in his *Art of Ringing* (1816) says:

'According to Parnell, the earliest artist and promoter of change ringing we have any account of, was Mr Fabian Stedman, born in the town of Cambridge, 1631. He introduced various peals on five and six bells, printing them on slips of paper (being by profession a printer). These, being distributed about the country, were soon brought to London; but what progress the art had made in the metropolis at this time does not appear. The Society of College Youths in the summer of 1657 on a visit to Cambridge, were presented by Mr Stedman with his peculiar production on five bells, since called Stedman's Principle, which was rung for the first time, at St Benet's Cambridge, and afterwards at a church on

College Hill, London [St Michael Royal], where the Society at that time usually practised, and from meeting at which place they obtained their name.'

Soon after this the Great Fire of 1666 demolished the church of St Michael and its bells. The church was rebuilt from Wren's designs and finished in 1694, but the lantern and turret which surmount the tower were not added till 1713. One would have thought that a peal of bells would have been installed, considering the associations of the old tower and bells with the early history of ringing. But only a single bell was hung, cast by John Hodson, in 1674; it was only 23 inches in diameter. Being cracked, it was recast in 1892.

It is indeed a strange irony that a City church, so intimately associated with the sound of bells – Dick Whittington's Church it is called because of his association with it – whose ancient peal was the first in scientific change ringing, should today be silent.

St Michael Royal is even now a blitzed ruin from the last war. Yet it still had something to say! It became a lunch-time meeting place for City office workers, and from among those who went there, in 1949, the Whittington Handbell Ringers were formed. Rehearsals were held in the church, but later, by permission of the Town Clerk of the City, Guildhall has been made their headquarters until St Michael Royal is built again.

The Whittington Handbell Ringers are under a Bell Master. Usually eight ringers are occupied, playing 16 bells. The total number of bells available for use is 17, which include C sharp and B flat and two F natural bells, high and low, for change of key. In the library of the Whittington Handbell Ringers are seventy or so arrangements of popular pieces, as well as specially written compositions. There are also a dozen or more carols, as well as children's songs, including the immortal 'Oranges and Lemons'.

Bell-ringing has moved forward enormously since the days of Edward II and Edward III. In those days there were comparatively few sequences of bells; bell-ringers were still experimenting with their craft. Methods had been tried out for striking the bells with the clappers from the inside and the outside, but they were liable to crack the bells, and failed to bring out the true tone.

Then came an important step forward – the swinging of the bell itself on pivots and sockets. The control and improvement of tone was enormous. A lever was attached to the stock on which the bell was mounted, while a rope from the end of the lever worked the bell from below. Later the lever was modified to a half or three-quarter wheel – later still a full wheel – with the rope lying in a grooved channel on the arc of the circle.

With this added facility in bell control, there came into practice the first call-changes, which were mostly the alteration in the sequence of two bells.

It would have seemed to have been to such a call-change that Dick Whittington (born 1358) halted his flight from London at Highgate when he heard the bells of St Mary-le-Bow rung to the rhythm:

'Turn a-gain Whit-ting-ton, thrice Lord Mayor of London.'

In May 1959 the bells of St Paul's rang a merry peal to celebrate the opening of the Mermaid Theatre at Puddle Dock. And with the merry peal a 'mermaid' appeared from the river to symbolise the occasion. Properly enough, the 'mermaid' was the daughter of a Liveryman – the only instance known in history! – he being Mr Jack Hawkins, actor, Citizen and Upholder of London. The opening show? 'Lock Up Your Daughters.'

At night there are other notes in the City. The chime that comes from Middle Temple Hall, followed immediately by the more sombre notes of the Law Courts. From St Clement Danes' the 'Oranges and Lemons' carillon, homely, nostalgic.

To the east one may hear faintly the note of a bugle. It comes from outside the City, from the Tower of London itself, and it contrasts strangely with the occasional sound of City bells, as it floats over the boundary. The Ceremony of the Keys! 'Whose Keys?' 'The Queen's Keys.' And then the Last Post, which marks the end of so many things. It is as poignant as the Lutine Bell at Lloyds, when it is struck once, to mark a ship that will never reach port.

CHAPTER 14

THE BARBICAN ARTS PLAN

When in 1833 the City Swordbearer recommended to the Court of Aldermen that the City's Waits had become utterly insignificant and that they had no functions or privileges, those poor shadows of a former musical greatness were quietly buried. An age of musical barrenness had settled in, and this was not greatly disturbed until the advent of Mr Weist Hill's Guildhall Orchestral Society.

It was this important amateur enterprise that became, as it were, the focus-point for the City's return to a positive sponsoring of music. Mr Weist Hill became the first Principal of the Guildhall School of Music, founded in 1880. Once more the City Corporation had actively identified itself with music, and has never again turned its back.

As we know, the Guildhall School of Music was an instant success, and the City's justification in taking such a non-commercial step was proved to the hilt, and pointed to the future.

Today the Barbican Scheme represents the apotheosis of the City's ideals, to be all that a great city should be – a place of residence for a full family life as well as being a place of commerce; to be a centre of the arts as well as a centre of trade.

In this great plan the City is both looking forward and looking back through the years. A mere 120 years ago the City of London had a resident population of 129,000; today it is in the region of 4,600. The Barbican Scheme is designed to bring back family life as well as cultural and artistic facilities, so as to create a full and balanced existence for something like 6,500 citizens as well as being a place of artistic recreation for those living outside.

The picture is precise. In the Barbican there will be 2,071 flats and maisonettes. There will be a theatre, a concert hall, an art gallery, a public library, and almost certainly a sculpture garden. The Guildhall School of Music and Drama, as well as the City of London School for Girls, will, so to speak, pick up their skirts and join forces with the new Art Centre, the cost of which, it is estimated, will be in the region of £10m. There will also be a hostel for students, there will be restaurants and public houses and shops. There will be massive garage space for cars at ground level, while above ground there will be raised walkways for pedestrians. In fact, traffic and pedestrians will be completely separated.

'We intend to bring back to the City a balanced existence, with music and the arts as much catered for as banking and commerce.' In those words Mr Eric Wilkins, C.B.E., Chairman of the Barbican Committee defined the aim of the project. 'Our first break-through in that direction was the Mermaid Theatre at Puddle Dock. Now, just as the City purchased two lungs for itself in the form of Epping Forest on the East and Burnham Beeches on the West, it is going about providing itself with a new heart.'

It is true to say that in one sense, by bringing citizens to live in the City, the clock is being turned back. In the early years of the nineteenth century the Barbican area was largely devoted to the textile trade. Business men lived with their families above their premises. With the increase of trade and the advent of the railway, business expanded and those resident City men gave up their living rooms on the first floor so that they might be turned into offices. Then they gave up the upper floors as well, and went to live outside the City. That was when the depopulation of the City took place.

Some people forget that so comparatively recently the City was residential, and it was from those that came the greatest opposition to a Barbican development other than a purely commercial one. But Mr Wilkins had his way.

For the record, it should be stated that Mr Wilkins was elected Chairman of the Barbican Committee in October 1957, and held that office until January 1963, when, no doubt due to the strain of piloting the Barbican project through its early stages, it seriously affected his health. He was succeeded by Alderman Sir Gilbert Inglefield, who held the office for four years. When Sir Gilbert resigned on account of his approaching Mayoralty, Mr Wilkins, by then fully recovered, resumed the Chairmanship.

In their ambitious plans to bring first-class music as a permanent feature to the City, the Barbican Committee are hoping that the Concert Hall will become the permanent home of the London Symphony Orchestra. Should this be achieved, as is likely, it will provide the City with a pattern of concert-going which has hitherto been completely absent.

By such an arrangement the London Symphony Orchestra would probably be able to provide a broadly based series of concerts over a thirty-four week season. In any one season there could also be seventeen or so recitals by well-known soloists, as well as several concerts by visiting British and foreign orchestras.

Standing just outside the north-west bastion of the Roman Wall is the historic pre-Wren Church of St Giles', Cripplegate. In their day, two printers who followed their trade in the Barbican area knew St Giles' intimately. They were also contemporaries of another local resident, the poet Milton. Their names, Condell and Hemming, make an instant appeal, for it was those men who first published twenty-two of Shakespeare's plays.

'If it had not been for Condell and Hemming,' observed Mr Wilkins, 'I think it is highly probable that we should not have Shakespeare today as we know him. The Barbican area is where

Shakespeare worked, and it is gratifying to know that the Barbican theatre is to become the permanent home of the Royal Shakespeare Company.

Slowly the wheel turns full circle; music is coming back to the City in strong flood. Music, of course, has never left the City. Today one has only to consider such fine organisations as the City Music Society, whose Chairman is Ivan Sutton, with their lunch-time concerts at the Bishopsgate Institute, the Celebrity Recitals at the Law Society's Common Room, the music to be heard at the Temple Church, the Church of the Holy Sepulchre, and St Paul's itself, to name but a handful, to show how strongly music and the love of music is entrenched in the Square Mile. Music has always been part of the City's daily life, but the new Arts Centre will be outstanding in this great City renaissance. Symphony concerts, Shakespeare, ballet – all the arts will be found there, at a centre the likes of which in terms of accessability is not to be found anywhere else in the world.

The London Waits departed with the last lingering London cries; music reached a low ebb in the hungry 'forties. But now the tide is flowing strongly, as if in response to Morley's: 'The ancient custome of this honourable and renouned Citie hath been ever to retaine and maintaine excellent and expert Musicians.' Those words might well be cut deeply over the portico of the Barbican Concert Hall.

Certainly the Barbican will bring back those words with renewed force, and it is thanks to the wisdom of those men of the City who, after the long fallow years when the violence of war had passed, formulated broad and bold plans that would restore the true heart of the City in the highest sense, as expressed in the City's motto:

'Domine Dirige Nos'.

INDEX